PEER COUNSELING SKILLS: A POCKET RESOURCE FOR PEER SUPPORT SPECIALISTS

PEER COUNSELING SKILLS: A POCKET RESOURCE FOR PEER SUPPORT SPECIALISTS

Charles Drebing, PhD

For information about permission to reproduce selections from this book, write to:

Alderson Press, LLC
4218 Wellington Drive
Fort Collins, CO 80526

Library of Congress Cataloging in Publication Data
Drebing, Charles, 1959–
Peer Counseling Skills: A Pocket Resource for Peer Support Specialists/ by Charles E. Drebing
ISBN 979-8-3302-5749-2

This book is dedicated to my prior supervisors: Walter Penk, Greg Binus, Craig Coldwell, and Sam Rofman, all of whom modeled a focused and disciplined dedication to the support of others, providing a wonderful model for me and many others to follow. I only ever saw them make decisions that reflected that the support of others was their top priority.

CONTENTS

ACKNOWLEDGMENTS

Special thanks to Heather Rodino and my wife, Susan Drebing, for their invaluable help in reviewing and improving this work. Thanks also to Rick Holland for his design work

.

HOW TO USE THIS BOOK

Peer counseling is a skill that takes years to learn to do well. You cannot develop that skill by simply sitting in a classroom. Like riding a bicycle, you have to do it in order to learn it.

Some people will naturally be better at counseling than others. Maybe you are one of those fortunate people. Others will struggle with it. If you are one of those people, know that there are plenty of other ways to support people. Even for those naturally good at peer counseling, it takes time and hard work to build the skills necessary to be helpful to the most people in the most effective ways.

People are generally quite poor at estimating how good they would be at peer counseling. Research shows that people greatly overestimate how good they would be as a counselor before they receive training. After good training, they often *underestimate* how good they are. It is only in getting real experience in peer counseling over time, and listening to feedback from clients and supervisors, that we get a more accurate perception of whether we are any good at it (Lepkowski, Packman, Smaby & Maddux, 2009).

Peer counseling is different from psychotherapy in very important ways. Both involve talking and listening in the context of helping relationships, but you want to be clear on what you are doing and not drift into psychotherapy. Psychotherapy requires a clinical license and typically focuses on specific "clinical" topics. Peer counseling typically focuses on a broader array of recovery and life issues, and relies on the shared experience of peer counselors. Both have a valuable role, but when it not clear which intervention is being provided, there can be bad outcomes for everyone. If you are working in a setting where psychotherapy is also offered, it will be particularly important for you to attend to the boundaries between the two. The National Practice Guidelines for Peer Specialists and Supervisors (2019) refer to "peer drift" as the natural but unfortunate tendency for the work of Peer Specialists to begin to resemble the work of clinician coworkers. This is a particular danger for peer counseling versus psychotherapy, as there is some natural overlap.

This book is designed to be an easy-to-access resource that you can keep with you and use while you are providing peer services. It is also designed to be a training resource for you as you learn this important skill. It is not a stand-alone training resource, as you'll want to include clinical supervision and classroom work to build your skills. In the following chapters you'll find general information about peer counseling. You'll also encounter exercises and questions to consider as you start peer counseling. Try to do these exercises. Answers for many of them are included in the back of the book—but don't just skip to the answers; try to formulate your own for each exercise and then look carefully at the differences and similarities between your answers and those supplied. That will help you build real skill.

It is important to acknowledge that I am not a Peer Support Specialist. I have personal experience of the impact of mental illness in my own life and in the lives of my family and friends, but I have not been employed as a peer counselor. This book reflects my own perspective as a mental health program manager and researcher. I have worked closely with many Peer Support Specialists while building recovery-oriented programs. I am convinced that the addition of Peer Support Specialists to mental healthcare is one of the most important developments of the past twenty years. Peer Support Specialists have added, and will hopefully continue to add, their own perspective to our understanding of peer counseling.

This book is not meant to replace more complete resources or education on Peer Support Specialist duties or services, and it is not a substitute for learning the guidelines and policies of the organization you work for. You will want to work closely with your supervisor and members of your treatment team as part of building your skills. Look for people who are good peer counselors and learn from them. They will be key supports as you begin the journey to develop these skills.

The field of peer support and the work of Peer Support Specialists is one of the most exciting developments in healthcare in the past 20 years. I don't think the field recognizes the way this new role is, and will continue to change how care is provided. I have created a blog to continue to discuss the range of issues tied to this new area of work **(https://www.charlesdrebing.com/peer-support-blog-3-1).** I invite you to look for posts that are relevant to your work and to let me know about any topics you'd like to see addressed.

CHAPTER 1

UNDERSTANDING PEER COUNSELING

Peer Support Specialists have a key role in helping others recover from clinical and life challenges. Their primary focus has been supporting adults with mental illness and substance use disorders, but that focus has been getting broader, as people and healthcare organizations recognize the value of peer support for a range of medical and mental health challenges.

Peer Support Specialists can provide support in multiple ways, including education, advocacy, practical support, community integration, and outreach. Through all these services, peer counseling is often a common element—maybe the most important—in what the Peer Support Specialist provides.

Peer counseling is a vague term that is poorly understood. There are many kinds of "counseling": career, pastoral, genetic, and even camp counseling. But what exactly is peer counseling? There are dangers in not being clear about what you are doing when you are "counseling." Healthcare in general involves organized treatment systems that include a large number of guidelines and carefully defined roles. As a peer counselor and/or a Peer Support Specialist, you will want to be organized as well. You want to know and be able to explain your role, including what you do and what you don't do. This will make it easier for other healthcare professionals to understand how to work with you, and it will be safer for you. There are always people willing to bring a lawsuit against anyone who might be to blame for something bad that happens to them. Healthcare has plenty of litigation. To the degree that you are clear on what your role is, and stick to that role, you will be much less likely to be a target of unfair complaints or lawsuits.

These definitions provide a good starting place:

Peer Support Specialist is an occupational title for a person who (1) has personal experience with a clinical or life problem such as a mental health and/or substance use disorder, and with recovery from that problem, and (2) is willing to talk about their experience in order to help others trying to recover from these or similar problems.

Peer support is a broad category of help provided by people with the same or similar problems or who are similar in some key respect (e.g., peer support between mothers or between veterans). Peer Support Specialists provide peer support, but many other people provide peer support as well.

Peer counseling is one type of peer support, and is defined as "counseling by an individual who has a status equal to that of the client, such as a college student trained to counsel other students or an employee trained to counsel coworkers" (*APA Dictionary of Psychology*, 2024). Note that this definition states that the peer counselor has (1) equal status with their client and (2) special training to provide the counseling. Counselor and client are specific and different roles—so this definition does not apply to two members of a peer support group who meet to mutually support each other. Peer counseling is more formal than that.

Peer counseling is one of the key services Peer Support Specialists provide, and this book is written with them in mind. While other people provide peer counseling and may benefit from this book, you'll see that the content is framed primarily for people who are employed as Peer Support Specialists providing peer counseling in a healthcare or social services setting.

Part of the challenge is the range of formats for peer counseling.

COMMON FORMATS IN WHICH PEER COUNSELING IS PROVIDED

1. **A Single Conversation.** You may meet someone and a casual conversation may lead to a discussion of a challenge they are facing. You may provide peer counseling in that conversation, and yet not see that person again.

2. **Ongoing Informal Conversations.** That single conversation may turn into a series of conversations in which you provide peer counseling. The opportunity to provide counseling over multiple meetings creates an opportunity for the counseling to have a larger and more lasting impact.

3. **Formal Peer Counseling.** As a Peer Support Specialist, you may be assigned clients whom you meet with on a regular basis to provide peer counseling. The purpose of the meetings is specifically focused on peer counseling and may be part of a number of services listed in that client's treatment plan.

PEER COUNSELING VS. PSYCHOTHERAPY

One of the most important distinctions to make in understanding peer counseling is the difference between peer counseling and psychotherapy. There are many overlapping qualities. For example, both peer counseling and psychotherapy emphasize listening and empathy. Both seek to help the client resolve problems.

Psychotherapy is an intervention provided by a select group of professionals with in-depth training in that intervention. We will refer to it as *psychotherapy*, but it may also be referred to as *therapy* or even simply as *counseling*. It typically has a more structured format than peer counseling and is governed by different rules and expectations. The following table lays out some of the key differences and commonalities.

Peer Counseling	Psychotherapy
Provided by a Peer Support Specialist or other person in a peer support role.	Provided by a licensed psychotherapist trained specifically in psychotherapy. These could be psychiatrists, psychologists, social workers, licensed mental health counselors, licensed marriage and family therapists, or nurse practitioners.
The credibility of the Peer Support Specialist is based on their personal experience with illness, treatment, and recovery.	The credibility of the psychotherapist is based on their graduate training and experience in providing psychotherapy.
Peer counseling emphasizes the fact that the provider and the client are peers—that	The psychotherapist and the client may have personal experience with the same problem, but this is not

they share the same or similar experiences.	emphasized and is often not talked about.
Because the credibility of the peer counselor is based on their personal experience, peer counseling always includes some self-disclosure by the peer counselor—and may include a lot.	Psychotherapy does include self-disclosure by the therapist, but this is relatively rare.
Peer counseling is provided in a range of settings in which peer support is appropriate.	Psychotherapy is provided in a clinical setting such as an outpatient clinic, private practice office, or an inpatient program.
The goals of peer counseling include providing mutual support to someone in a way that encourages their recovery.	The goals of psychotherapy include helping the person address a specific clinical problem(s) by helping them gain insight into themselves or their situation, and thus change their behavior or environment.
Peer counseling can include a variety of interactions, ranging from brief conversations in the hallway to ongoing individual meetings over extended periods of time.	Psychotherapy usually takes place in a private office and in specific sessions, most of which are one hour long.
Peer counseling includes a variety of interactions, some very short and others lengthy. It is not typically reimbursed as a specific intervention by most insurance companies.	Psychotherapy is a specific intervention, typically provided in thirty- or fifty-minute increments. It is recognized and paid for by most insurance companies and other sources of funding.

Peer counseling can help people address a wide range of life problems that may or may not be secondary to a diagnosed disorder. Peer counseling does not focus primarily on a disorder.	Psychotherapy usually focuses on issues tied to a specific diagnosed disorder.
Peer counseling usually focuses on problems that the client wants to talk about. The peer counselor may bring up issues for discussion, but the client raises most topics.	Psychotherapy often goes more deeply into the client's problem, drawing the client into a discussion of underlying and less-conscious experience and feelings that they may not be aware of.
Peer counseling often involves the peer counselor connecting the client to other people, such as another peer support provider, people in the community, or even a new healthcare provider.	Psychotherapists may refer clients to other providers, but they rarely introduce clients to other people in the community.
Peer counseling may involve going with the client into the community to meet other people or accompanying them while they participate in a community-based group or activity.	Psychotherapy rarely involves any activity in the community, and when it does, it is tied directly to the psychotherapy protocol.
Both emphasize listening to and having empathy, respect, and positive regard for the client.	
Both the peer counselor and psychotherapist are responsible for similar ethical and professional guidelines, including the expectation of protecting the privacy of clients, the respect for professional and personal boundaries, and the avoidance of conflicts of interest.	

Both encourage the client to solve their own problems and to take responsibility for the solution.
Both involve mutual give-and-take, with the Peer Support Specialist and the psychotherapist also learning and benefiting from the experience. This may be more openly discussed in peer counseling, but it is present in both.
Peer counselors and psychotherapists are typically part of a larger clinical team, and so both recognize the need to collaborate with other helpers working with the client.

THE RISKS FOR PEER SUPPORT SPECIALISTS WHEN THEY DRIFT INTO PSYCHOTHERAPY

Psychotherapy is a clinical but also a legal term, and it is tied to specific jobs with specific training. If Peer Support Specialists provide peer counseling that actually meets the criteria for psychotherapy, they are not acting in line with the community's expectations of their role, which creates legal vulnerability for the Peer Support Specialists. These roles are carefully regulated, and the Peer Specialist, as well as the organization they work for, can be vulnerable to legal action if they are providing a service they are not trained to do, and are not permitted to do under the law. The Peer Support Specialist is also violating the expectations of the other clinicians they work with. This will quickly undermine the trust of those partners, who will not want to work with a Peer Support Specialist who is not careful about professional roles and boundaries.

Psychotherapists have years of graduate training focusing on how to provide psychotherapy. When peer counseling crosses the line into psychotherapy, the person providing the counseling is moving past their formal training. They may have experience as a client in psychotherapy, but that is not the same as being trained to be a psychotherapist. You don't want to be working beyond the range of your skills and/or training.

If the welfare of our clients is our top priority, we should be concerned anytime that we find ourselves providing any services that we are not adequately trained for. Otherwise, before we know it, we can end up in very complex conversations in which we can't provide the support the other person needs.

IS PEER COUNSELING SECOND BEST?

The answer is a resounding **no**! Peer counseling and psychotherapy are two different but complementary tools that each have a valuable role in helping people recover. A great deal of research shows that psychotherapy can help people reduce clinical symptoms. Peer counseling has developed more recently as a formal service, and so there is less research on its benefits—but the research that has begun to accrue shows that peer counseling also helps people recover.

Peer counseling and psychotherapy do not compete. In fact, the current research suggests that they complement each other. For example, if we look at the studies that evaluate services that include psychotherapy and peer support, it is clear that people who used clinical care showed clear improvement. People who used 12-step and other peer support groups also showed clear improvement (Kaskutas, 2009; Houlston et al., 2011; Kennedy et al., 2007). Those who used both at the same time improved more than those who used either treatment alone or peer support alone (Pagano et al., 2013; Kelly et al., 2010).

That doesn't mean that some psychotherapists do not feel intimidated by peer counseling or feel the need to act like their work is more important than yours. Many people are competitive by nature and feel the need to communicate their conviction that they are more important than others. Comments from clinical partners about whose work is more important is an unfortunate waste of time and does not typically merit a response. Over time, I've seen many clinicians change their views of the value of peer support and peer counseling as they get more experience in working with Peer Support Specialists, and more opportunities to see their clients improve because of good peer counseling. Arguing with those clinicians never seems to help, but doing good work is almost always persuasive.

WHAT YOU BRING AS A PEER SUPPORT SPECIALIST

Credibility. Because of your shared experience with your clients, you have a type of credibility that clinicians typically do not have, and you are often able to develop early trust with clients.

Connectability. Establishing a sense of connection between the client and the helper is typically critical in both peer counseling and psychotherapy. Because the client sees you as more like them due to your personal experience, they will often find you easier to relate to than a psychotherapist and so that connection will develop more quickly.

Information About the Experience of Illness, Care, and Recovery. Your personal experience provides you with a knowledge of both illness and recovery from that illness. Most clinicians do not have that personal experience. They may have studied these topics in books and have personal experience with some form of illness and with helping people with those disorders, but their limited personal experience is still an important disadvantage. Even those clinicians who do have relevant personal experience will not often talk about it with their clients. Training for psychotherapy usually emphasizes that psychotherapists do not talk about their personal experiences except in very specific situations. In contrast, Peer Support Specialists must talk about their experience if they are to actually be a "peer."

A Different Voice. The peer counselors I work with have helped me see that peer counselors tend to say different things to their clients and say them in a different way than psychotherapists do. This is due in part to their different perspective on recovery. Clients also trust peers in a different way. Whatever the reason, the input from peer counselors is different—it may push the client to take personal responsibility, it may bring in topics like spirituality that most psychotherapists are hesitant to talk about, and it may focus on more practical or immediate aspects of recovery. Peer counselors should be proud of their different voice and perspective and protect and nurture it.

Additional Connections. Peer counselors typically have an array of relationships with other people in recovery that can be of great help to the client. Again, this complements the types of connections that psychotherapists have—which usually include other formal healthcare providers and services. In contrast, peer counselors are often more able to connect clients with other peers, other peer support groups, and other resources in the community.

A FINAL NOTE ON PEER COUNSELING AND PSYCHOTHERAPY

Good peer counseling helps clients make more progress in their psychotherapy. They are more hopeful, and more active in thinking about their problems and recovery. They feel more supported and so are more willing to take the risk of looking openly at challenging topics. Psychotherapists will find that clients who also engage in good peer counseling will talk more openly, move more quickly to solve problems, and be more optimistic about their own recovery.

Likewise, good psychotherapy helps clients make more progress in their peer counseling. Many people have problems and experiences that make it difficult to connect to others, including peers. Progress in psychotherapy can improve clients' ability to connect to others and so to benefit from peer counseling. I see many clients moving from psychotherapy to peer counseling and peer support groups, as they are better able to trust others and talk openly about their recovery.

Close collaboration between peer counselors and psychotherapists is already growing and is a future area of specialization for Peer Support Specialists.

CHAPTER 2

BASIC QUALITIES OF A HELPING RELATIONSHIP

Peer counseling is provided within the context of a relationship. It may be a brand-new relationship, but the relationship creates the setting in which the peer counseling can happen. If the counseling is to be successful, that relationship should have some key common elements.

UNCONDITIONAL POSITIVE REGARD

Positive regard is a formal term that refers to the fact that you, as a peer counselor, need to take a stance of caring about, and respect for, the person you are counseling. *Unconditional* means that your caring is not tied to any quality they have or anything they do. No matter who they are and what they've done in the past, you hold them in high regard and care about their welfare.

Often, our own experience of caring and respect from other people is conditional—based on some characteristic of who we are or something we do. Unfortunately, conditional regard creates a setting in which clients feel that they need to do or be something in order to gain that support. You want your clients to feel that your support has no requirements or expectations—you care about them no matter what.

This is not easy. Some clients come with unattractive qualities, and some do, or have done, things that we may dislike or even feel repelled by. Here we want to remember the old distinction: you can like the person and dislike their behavior.

Unconditional positive regard will take work on your part. The capacity to truly care about others unconditionally does not come naturally to most of us, but with work, we can do it. Consider the following suggestions:

1. Think about people in your life who have provided unconditional positive regard to you and/or to others. What did they do, and how did they do it? Reflect on them frequently as models for your work.

2. When thinking about your clients, distinguish between the person and their qualities. Their qualities may be in part due to genetics, the family they were raised in, and their experience. Behind that is the person you want to serve.

3. Similarly, when thinking about your clients, distinguish between the person and their actions. Their actions will typically reflect their past experience, the patterns of behavior that have developed over years of positive and negative experience, and the mental illness that they are struggling with. Their behaviors reflect them but are not them.

4. Develop your reasons for caring about people in general. These may be philosophical or spiritual in nature. Some

peer counselors focus on the value of all persons. Some focus on the value of the person's potential—whom they could become. Some look for positive aspects of each client and focus their caring on those positive aspects. Still others think about the person they themselves were before they recovered.

5. Remind yourself of those reasons frequently as a way to prompt that regard. You want to feel that regard and communicate it to your clients directly and indirectly.

6. Track how well you are providing unconditional regard to clients. Whom do you show this to, and whom do you struggle to provide it to?

7. Identify patterns of when you are able and not as able to provide that regard, and look for ways to build that capacity.

8. Talk with others about your efforts, where you are successful and where you are less successful. Find others who are working on this as well, and collaborate in finding ways to improve your ability to give unconditional positive regard.

9. Identify any situations in which you consistently are not able to give unconditional regard. Some peer counselors find that they have great difficulty feeling and communicating care to clients with specific behaviors, such as people who have committed crimes or are abusive toward others. As a peer counselor, you want to be able to work with everyone. Over time you may find that you cannot do this—and so will want to be clear with yourself and others about whom you are not able to work with. If you cannot act toward some clients in a way

that communicates a reasonable level of unconditional positive regard, it is better to help that person find another peer counselor.

EMPATHY

Empathy is the capacity to understand the experience of another person. When a peer counselor feels empathy with a client's experience, and is able to communicate that empathy, clients feel understood. They feel the peer counselor grasps something about their experience, and that shared understanding does several key things:

1. It helps the client continue talking, knowing that the peer counselor understands what they have been talking about.

2. It helps the client feel connected to the peer counselor, as they feel the peer has joined in the understanding.

3. It helps the client feel that their experience has been validated. That doesn't mean that you approve of the experience but simply that you understand it as they experienced it.

4. It gives the peer counselor insight and information about the client that is likely to be important in helping them. Knowing the external facts of an experience and actually understanding that experience from the inside are two different things. When a peer counselor truly empathizes with a client's experience, they gain a greater amount of information than the simple facts.

5. It encourages the client to go deeper. In the process of peer counseling, people often talk about things that they only partially understand. When a peer counselor communicates empathy, the client feels that someone is

with them in trying to understand their experience—they feel accompanied in the task of thinking through their problem. That sense of being accompanied by someone else makes it easier to keep talking and to look at issues that may feel too difficult to explore alone.

Like unconditional positive regard, empathy is also a complex ability that takes time and effort to develop. It is not easy to improve your ability to empathize with others and to improve how we communicate that empathy, but here are a few strategies:

1. Given that empathy is the ability to understand others' experience, you will want to spend lots of time listening to others, particularly those with experiences different from yours. We all tend to naively assume that people are similar to us in their views, and how their internal world works. After many years of working with clients, it is clear to me that no two people are the same. Every person is unique, and the differences are often surprising. If we just take the time to listen closely enough to recognize the differences, we will stop making wrong assumptions about other people. Become a student of the differences: listen to people as they talk about their lives, their explanations about why they do what they do, why they feel the ways they feel. Start with the assumption that everyone is different.

2. Books and movies often have a goal of giving the audience a glimpse of someone else's experience or perspective. Actively use books and films to expand your understanding of the variety of people's experience. Find opportunities to talk about films and books with others who may have different perspectives on them. Look for books and films that may stretch your comfort zone.

3. Become more aware of your own background—how it has shaped your view of yourself, others, and the world. This can be done in a range of ways—spending time reflecting on your experience, writing in a journal about it, making a concerted effort to talk more openly about yourself with those around you who are good listeners, or using your own peer counseling and/or psychotherapy to better understand yourself. The more we understand our own uniqueness, the more we tend to appreciate and respect the differences in others.

CONGRUENCE

The term *congruence* refers to the quality of being genuine—being the "real you" in your interactions with others. Congruence requires that you are aware of how you feel and what you think. It may seem simple, but it is not. We are all complex people with mixed and, at times, contradictory feelings, only some of which are easy to recognize. It takes time and effort to recognize all of our feelings and thoughts, and to keep track of them in a way so that our self-awareness is fairly high.

Congruence also requires that the client can see who we are. This does not mean that we have to share all our feelings all the time with our clients. It does mean that clients can see who we are as people and that what they see is genuine. We have all developed ways of defending ourselves from the scrutiny of others. These often have become second nature—we don't even see when we are using them. To be congruent, we'll want to be more aware of our defenses and turn them off when it helps our clients see us more clearly.

We have all seen people who are acting in a way that we could describe as "fake," often in an effort to create an impression. Think about how you respond to people when they are acting in a "fake" manner. I often have a very negative response, tending to keep my distance. I also find myself trying to guess why they are acting in this way: What are they hiding? What is their real agenda? You can imagine that this would not be helpful for a client to be wondering about you as a peer counselor. That is wasted time and energy that they need to be spending on solving their own problem. Being genuine leaves your client feeling like he or she understands how you feel and who you are, and that they can trust that if you have any specific concerns or feelings, you will bring them up.

You also want to be congruent as a model to clients. Many of the problems that clients bring to peer counselors have something to do with not being aware of their feelings or not communicating their real feelings to others. Being honest with ourselves and others about how we really think and feel is a general challenge for everyone. There is some risk involved, and so it takes courage to be genuine. In contrast, being ungenuine can lead to a wide range of problems: poor communication, feeling distant from others, and feeling a lack of direction. Modeling congruence to clients gives them the message that it is healthy and desirable to be genuine with people you trust.

Congruence also takes time and effort to develop. As with positive regard and empathy, we all start with different levels of congruence, depending on our background experiences and models. All peer counselors will want to increase their ability to be aware of their thoughts and feelings, and to communicate these when appropriate. There are many strategies for improving congruence, but here are a few simple ones:

1. **Do a Self-Assessment of How Congruent You Are.** How aware are you of what you are feeling and thinking? We are often not good judges of our own awareness, and so it is important to get feedback from others who know us well and who we trust to tell us the truth.

2. **Find Ways to Increase Awareness of Your Own Feelings.** Develop a routine of asking yourself how you are feeling several times a day. You may want to track your feelings using a journal.

3. **Expand Your Vocabulary to Describe Your Feelings.** There are some common guides to feeling words that many have found helpful in expanding their ability to recognize their own feelings; you can find them on Amazon or other sites. Try to use different words and phrases to more accurately describe your feelings to yourself and to others.

4. **Increase Your Efforts to Communicate What You Are Actually Feeling in Daily Life.** Of course, this strategy assumes you have people you trust to handle that information. Even with people who are trustworthy, we often tend to play it safe and report less of what we think and feel than would be helpful. Consciously choosing to say more on a regular basis will increase general congruence over time.

5. **Increase the Number of People You Know Who Can Be Trusted to Hear, Respect, and Even Appreciate Knowing More About What You Feel and Think.** The more you surround yourself with this type of person, the easier it is to be yourself. Similarly, it may be worth considering how to reduce your contact with those who are not trustworthy in respecting your individual thoughts and feelings. The more time each day you spend being more of your "real self," the more likely you will do that fully with your clients.

TRUSTWORTHINESS

Trust is the foundation of an effective peer counseling relationship. The client's trust in you depends on their ability to trust others as well as the degree to which you appear to be trustworthy. While clients often have to work to trust others, you also want to work to be as trustworthy as possible. It is smart for clients not to trust a peer counselor who does not appear trustworthy, and so your success will depend on your ability to communicate the fact that you are genuinely trustworthy.

Issues of trust often focus on genuineness, empathy, and positive regard, so if you can build those qualities, you will greatly improve your trustworthiness. Trust also involves several other key areas:

1. Are you consistent? Do you approach your work and your clients in the same way over time?
2. Are you reliable? Do you follow through on what you say?
3. Are you committed and persistent? Will you give up on them?

Consistency often develops as new peer counselors get comfortable with their work and build their skill level. Experienced peer counselors approach their work with professionalism—they want to be as consistent and focused in each case so that they have the best outcome for every client. Like any professional, a peer counselor has a set of skills and applies those skills in a systematic way. You don't want to do good work only when you feel inspired or motivated, and then do mediocre work when you don't. Professionals seek to do a good job every time, not just when they feel like it. Clients can tell when peer counselors act like professionals and when they act like amateurs.

Following through on what you say is one of the most important actions you can take to build trust. Many people, including many peer counselors, are tempted to say they will do things that will help. When it comes to actually taking the time and effort to follow through, many people simply don't measure up. Clients will track your follow-through very closely. One failure to follow through will change the trust level and the relationship significantly. We all mess up at times, but given the importance of follow-through, any failure requires a genuine apology and discussion if future trust is to be saved.

Here are some strategies for building trustworthiness:

1. **Get Feedback from Others.** Again, you don't know what you don't know. You may not be aware of how trustworthy you really are. Ask those people you trust to tell you the truth about your trustworthiness.

2. **Track What You Say You Will Do and Your Follow-Up.** You should be able to see clearly any patterns in your follow-up.

3. **Routinely Repair Any Breaches in Trust.** You will absolutely drop the ball at times—it is what you do when that happens that is important. Repairing breaches in trust is part of your work, and you want to get good at that.

Get good at apologizing too. You will make mistakes despite your best efforts, and so your response will mean the difference between a break in trust and what can be a positive experience. How you respond to your mistakes is the key.

There are genuine apologies that repair trust, and then there are a variety of ways to apologize that don't work. You can see it when politicians get caught doing something they are not proud of. Their apologies often are forced, and fall in a few predictable categories that explain why they don't help (Molinsky, 2016). An effective apology typically includes the following elements: (1)

taking responsibility for your role in a situation or event, (2) expressing regret, (3) asking forgiveness, and (4) explaining how it won't happen again. Ineffective apologies take several common forms:

- **The Empty Apology.** It's what you say to someone when you know you need to apologize but are so annoyed or frustrated that you can't muster any real feeling to put behind it. It is an apology in word only.

- **The Excessive Apology.** An apology is supposed to acknowledge responsibility and seek to repair the situation. The excessive apology emphasizes that you feel badly but does not repair the situation. Your actions to repair things will go much further to build trust than saying "I'm so sorry!" over and over again.

- **The Incomplete Apology.** In this situation, the apology does not have all of the elements. It may include regret but no responsibility. It may include taking responsibility but nothing about how you will avoid the mistake in the future. All of the elements are needed.

- **The Denial.** This is not an apology and often destroys trust in a way that is hard to recover. Be very slow to deny any fault until you're sure you have no part in a problem.

Recognize and take pride in being trustworthy. It is one of the great tasks of working with people. Feel good as you achieve greater degrees of trustworthiness.

RECOGNITION OF—AND RESPECT FOR—DIFFERENCES

We all at times are tempted to see the world only through our own eyes, forgetting that we as individuals are unique, as is everyone else. When peer counselors make the mistake of assuming that their clients see the world like they do, they start to create misunderstandings that can lead to mistrust

Effective peer counselors recognize and respect the differences they see in their clients, and in themselves. They know that these variations are associated with differences in perspectives, values, and behaviors. They recognize that understanding the client's perspective is central to their work, and so they actively look for, and support, those differences.

While clients and counselors can be different in a myriad of ways, a few large categories are worth special attention:

1. **Age.** Our physical age has key implications for every aspect of the peer counseling process. Physical development, emotional development, and social roles are all directly related to physical age, and so the type of work that will be done in peer counseling will be very different depending on the client's age. Counseling someone who is sixteen is often quite different from counseling someone who is twenty. An effective peer counselor should have some sense of the typical patterns in psychological and social functioning associated with age. A good class in developmental psychology is one way to build that background.

   We all make assumptions about others based on age, and those assumptions can include biases that impact the peer counseling process. If we assume, for example, that all people over the age of sixty are less active and have fewer goals for their lives, we are likely to misunderstand some of our clients. As with all areas of difference, your responsibility as a peer counselor is to be familiar with patterns typically associated with common differences, but to be always attentive to ways that your specific client fits or does not fit those patterns.

We must also be aware of how we are impacted by our own areas of difference. Our own age will have an impact on how we see clients. The match or mismatch between your age and your client's age may lead you, or your client, to make assumptions that, again, hurt the peer counseling process. Be attentive to these temptations, and be willing to talk about them with your clients if you want to avoid making assumptions that undercut your work.

2. **Culture/Subculture.** *Culture* is defined by the *Merriam-Webster Dictionary* as "the customary beliefs, social forms, and material traits of a racial, religious, or social group."

    Increasingly, people from a single country can represent a number of different cultures or subcultures. Sometimes this reflects the fact that their parents moved to that country from a different place and culture. Sometimes, differences in cultures simply represent the variations that exist within a single country.

    Working with cultural differences between clients has a number of advantages in a peer counseling setting. Counselors who recognize those differences and communicate their recognition to their clients will be able to more quickly understand the experience and values of their clients, and will be more likely to be seen by those clients as understanding and respectful.

3. **Race.** *Race* is defined as "any one of the groups that humans are often divided into based on physical traits regarded as common among people of shared ancestry."

We often confuse racial and cultural differences, as both often occur together. Racial differences can be associated with differences in experience within a culture. The experience of African Americans versus Native Americans in the United States has been quite different, for example, and those differences in experience impact the way members of those groups understand themselves and approach peer counseling.

Considerable research suggests that when counselors and clients are from the same racial group, the trust develops more quickly and positive outcomes are more likely. This makes sense, as clients are more likely to feel understood more quickly. The research also indicates that when counselors and clients are from different racial groups, the work can be successful, but it is slower and the counselor must make an additional effort to build trust.

4. **Religion and Personal Philosophy.** *Religion* is defined as "a personal set or institutionalized system of religious attitudes, beliefs, and practices."

Not everyone belongs to an organized religion, but those who do tend to feel that it would be helpful to be able to talk about their religion and religious concerns in counseling settings (Finlayson Smith, 2007). Interestingly, they tend to be concerned that their counselors will not understand or respect their beliefs. As with all other areas of difference, clients are worried that counselors may not respect them and cannot understand those differences.

Everyone has a personal philosophy, whether they recognize it or not. Personal philosophies represent a set of values and beliefs about life and how it works, which guides the client's larger decisions. A personal philosophy may be conscious or less than conscious. It may be consistent or inconsistent with the explicit views of an organized religion that the client belongs to. We often learn our personal philosophies from our families and our experience in life, and so there is endless variety.

Working with clients with different religious and personal philosophies can be a particular challenge in peer counseling. By their very nature, religions and philosophies make claims about what is ultimately true and valuable. Talking with someone who has a different view from ours as to what is ultimately true can make us feel like we need to convince them that our views are correct. While this urge is understandable, it does not help and often ruins the peer counseling process.

Clients never enter peer counseling because they want to exchange their religious or philosophical views for those of someone else. They experience counselors who want to change their religious or philosophical views as disrespectful and uncaring. The basis of a successful peer counseling relationship is respect, and so counselors must work hard to recognize and value the differences in everyone in this important area of life, to develop an abiding respect for those differences, and to recognize and avoid their own temptation to try to change their client's religious or philosophical views to match their own.

5. **Sex.** Biological sex is a key difference in people that is determined by anatomy, physiology, genetics, and hormones. All animals, including humans, have a sex, which is usually categorized as male or female, though there are variations. Sex is often confused with gender.

6. **Gender.** Gender-role identity is associated with biological sex but has some key differences. It includes the notion of social and cultural aspects of gender. There are behaviors that we see as "masculine" or "feminine". People have values and beliefs, often associated with culture and our background, about the different genders; some of these are conscious, but many are often unconscious.

   Differences between peer counselors and clients in gender-role identity, and in the way we see gender, can be a challenge to developing a successful peer counseling relationship. As in each of these areas of potential difference, peer counselors need to educate themselves on gender, and particularly on their own personal assumptions and values related to it. The goal is to recognize the variations that clients will have and to recognize the peer counselor's own biases and assumptions so that the peer can better understand and respect the client.

7. **Sexual Orientation.** *Sexual orientation* is defined by the APA as the "often enduring pattern of emotional, romantic, and/or sexual attractions to men, women, or both." You and your client each bring your own sexual orientation to the peer counseling situation, including whom you are naturally attracted to, your past experiences with being attracted to others, and how others have responded to you. While there has been a lot of cultural change in how sexual orientation is seen, individuals still have a wide range of feelings about differences in this area, and these differences are important to understand and appreciate.

In a peer counseling situation in which your sexual orientation is different from your client's, you want to be sure you are well educated about those differences and recognize what concerns the client may feel about those differences. As with any area of difference, you want to be ready to talk about it openly if your client feels the need. Some clients may feel no need to talk about it, while others may not be able to start peer counseling without first clarifying what you know and feel about the difference between you and your client. They are usually looking to see whether you recognize and respect how they are different in order to determine if they can and should trust you as a counselor.

8.   **Marital Status.** Whether a client is single, cohabitating, married, divorced, or widowed will have very important implications for their lives. Counselors who understand these potential differences are more able to communicate understanding of the client and to anticipate supports and barriers to recovery. Like with all aspects of culture, marital status is changing, with more couples cohabitating and more people choosing not to get married or to get married at an older age. Differences between the peer counselor and the client, in terms of marital status and views about it, can represent a barrier to understanding and trust building.

9.   **Disability.** There are a range of disabilities, but clients with some of the more obvious or more limiting ones will have a clear sense of being different from others. This may be based on their experience with the disability itself or on how others treat them. Western culture has been increasingly inclusive of members with significant disabilities, yet there is a long way to go.

If you have a disability, be aware of how it has impacted your experience and how that experience colors your peer counseling. Also be aware of how clients may respond to you if they know about your disability. When you see clients with disabilities, be aware that you may need to do some quick study to find out about how that disability typically impacts others. More importantly, be attuned to how that client sees that disability and what it may mean for them as they approach peer counseling.

10. **Financial Status.** Financial resources have a significant impact on mental health and recovery. People with fewer financial resources are more likely to have mental health problems and a greater need for treatment. Unfortunately, their lack of resources makes it less likely they will be able to participate in peer counseling or other clinical care. When they do participate, they are more likely to drop out. When they do complete treatment, they are less likely to have a successful outcome (Thompson, Goldberg & Nielsen, 2018).

There has not been good research on how differences in the financial resources of clients versus counselors impact the work. Given the correlation of financial resources with so many other variables like race, work experience, and trauma, it seems very likely that differences in financial background may become a barrier in the peer counseling conversations. Counselors should be curious about clients' financial resources and how their resources have colored their experience.

11. **Rural vs. Urban vs. Suburban.** Where our clients live and where they were raised have a great impact on how they approach peer counseling. Adults who live and/or were raised in rural areas are less likely to participate in

any form of mental health treatment, and when they do, it is less likely to be specialized mental healthcare and less likely to be the more effective evidence-based forms of care (Hauenstein et al., 2006). This appears to be due to a number of situational factors, but does include the tendency for adults from rural backgrounds to value self-reliance highly and to avoid asking for help from anyone.

Whether your client is from an urban, suburban, or rural setting, you'll want to be curious about how that impacts their experience and how they see the counseling. If you have a different background from your client, look for opportunities to better understand their experience.

12. **Veteran Status.** Because of factors such as background variables that predict who enlists in the military, the process by which the military chooses whom to accept, and the active-healthy lifestyle that is promoted in the military, veterans tend to be healthier than their civilian counterparts when it comes to physical health, mental health, academic and vocational success, and life span (Sullivan-Baca, Rehman & Haneef, 2023). This may be surprising, given the media attention often given to veterans with mental health conditions like PTSD, but research shows that veteran status is associated with a number of positive factors. Veterans tend to be more engaged in their communities, to be more likely to know and to help their neighbors, and to volunteer in their communities.

If you are not a veteran and find yourself working with a client who is, you will want to talk with them about their experience and how it has impacted their life. Veterans often like to work clinically with other veterans, but this is often not possible, given the small number of clinicians who are veterans. Combat is a unique experience that veterans may have been through. Be sure to inquire about that experience. If they have that in their background, be attentive to the risks for trauma and other mental health issues that are associated with combat experience.

A FINAL NOTE ON THESE QUALITIES

Respect for differences, empathy, congruence, and unconditional positive regard are broad concepts that can be difficult to fully understand. Many people new to peer counseling underestimate the power of these qualities, preferring to move on to more active strategies like advice giving and confrontation. Experienced peer counselors know that it is respect, empathy, congruence, and unconditional positive regard that do most of the heavy lifting in the peer counseling situation. Without them, you will have difficulty establishing and maintaining helping relationships with most clients. With them, many of your clients will start to make changes regardless of what other peer counseling techniques you use.

By embodying these qualities, you are modeling these behaviors for your clients. Most clients will not have these qualities—they often are not congruent, are not empathetic, don't have positive regard in an unconditional way, and don't fully respect difference in others. Most importantly for the peer counseling situation, they typically do not act these ways toward themselves. You, as the peer counselor, are modeling these behaviors for them. Most clients who participate in peer counseling over time will become more empathic toward others, more able to feel unconditional regard for themselves, and so more able to recognize and respect the individual person they are and be more congruent.

To further build these qualities in yourself, take some time to complete the following self-evaluation. Think about what you've seen in your own behavior and any feedback you've gotten from others you trust. Try to give as accurate of a rating as possible. When you are done, select two dimensions to target for improvement. Write down a goal for each and a plan for how to improve that dimension. Talk with your supervisor and/or peer mentor about these areas and your plan.

EXERCISE 1: SELF-EVALUATION

Rate yourself below on these key peer counseling dimensions by circling the number that best describes your common behavior toward other people.

Unconditional Positive Regard
1   2   3   4   5   6   7   8   9   10
Never   Sometimes   Always
Empathy
1   2   3   4   5   6   7   8   9   10
Never   Sometimes   Always
Congruence
1   2   3   4   5   6   7   8   9   10
Never   Sometimes   Always
Trustworthiness
1   2   3   4   5   6   7   8   9   10
Never   Sometimes   Always
Respectful of Individual Differences
1   2   3   4   5   6   7   8   9   10
Never   Sometimes   Always

Plan for further development: Choose one or two dimensions above that you want to improve on. Set a goal and plan below for each.
Goal 1: Improve on the dimension of _______________________ Plan:
Goal 2: Improve on the dimension of _______________________ Plan:

CHAPTER 3

BASIC SIGNS OF EFFECTIVE PEER COUNSELING

Peer counseling primarily involves conversation, and effective conversations follow common patterns that you will want to be watching for. The focus of the conversation may vary, depending on what the client is concerned about, but you want to recognize the basic signs of a conversation that is going in a good direction versus when the conversation has gotten off track and requires some extra work to get it back on track.

SIGN #1: THE FOCUS IS ON THE CLIENT

Effective peer counseling maintains a focus on the client and their concern(s). This is very different from the typical conversations we have each day with friends and acquaintances. In those conversations, we typically share the focus of attention, shifting back and forth between talking about ourselves and our concerns and then focusing on the others in the discussion. Effective peer counseling situations are very different in that the sole purpose is to help the client, and so the focus of the discussion is almost always on them, and even when it is not, it is always in the service of the client.

One very concrete sign that the focus is on the client is that they talk more than the peer counselor. Effective peer counselors know that clients need to do most of the talking. This reflects the reality that clients need to explain a lot about their situation and their experience, and that they typically benefit more from talking than listening to others.

Keeping the focus on the client takes discipline. Many inexperienced peer counselors will consciously or unconsciously use the peer counseling situation to talk about themselves. They may take up time telling clients about their opinions and experiences in a way that brings the attention back to them. They may not even recognize that they are using the client and the peer counseling to get their own needs for attention met. While there are situations in which counselors should talk about their experiences and views, doing so should not take the focus away from the client and the shared effort to solve their problem.

SIGN #2: THE CLIENT IS RESPONSIBLE FOR THEIR LIFE—WE RESPECT THEIR ROLE

If you listen in on most conversations between two people who are working together, you will quickly be able to tell their relative roles—who feels responsible for what happens. In an effective peer counseling setting, the counselor always communicates that the client is responsible for their life and their decisions.

The message that they are responsible is apparent in many ways. It can be communicated directly through statements by the counselor affirming that the client is responsible for what is discussed and how the conversation goes. More often, it is communicated indirectly. For example, it can be communicated by questions: "What do you want to do in this situation?" "What do you want to see happen?" "What direction do you want to take this in?" It can be communicated by waiting for the client to start the discussion about the problem they want to solve, instead of the counselor starting to talk about what they think the client should work on. It can be communicated by reminding clients who keep looking for advice that you can offer your experience, but they must make a decision for themselves.

Some clients may try to avoid feeling responsible. They may be uncomfortable about solving their own problems and/or even determining the direction of the peer counseling. They may act in a way that makes you feel that you need to take responsibility, or that subtly pressures you lead the discussion. For example, they may resist setting a direction for the peer counseling or stating what they want to accomplish. They may treat you as though you have the answers to their problems, and if only you would tell them what to do, they would feel better. They may act as though no one is responsible. These behaviors often tell you how they approach problems and possibly how they approach life. Most importantly, they represent a barrier to successful peer counseling.

If the client acts as though the counselor has all the answers, and the counselor inadvertently starts to act like they do have the answers and so are responsible for the peer counseling, the counselor has just undercut their ability to help. You want to be tenacious about maintaining the stance that your client is responsible for solving their problem. Your job is to help them figure out what they want to do, but you cannot be the one who chooses the right solution for them, and you are not ultimately responsible for the outcome.

In general, advice-giving by the counselor undercuts the message that the client is responsible. You can offer information or suggestions, but be careful not to do this in a way that suggests you are responsible. Consider the difference between two statements by a counselor: "I think you should end that friendship" and "What are your thoughts about whether you should take the step toward ending that friendship?" The first suggests that the counselor has analyzed the problem and knows the best solution. The client can say, "My counselor told me I should end that friendship," suggesting that the client feels that the counselor has responsibility for the decision. The second statement invites discussion but, more importantly, affirms that it is the client's thoughts that are important—it is the client who will make this decision.

Peer counselors may have a great deal of experience and knowledge that could be helpful to clients. Often, that information is not as helpful as we imagine, and yet there are times when we want to share something that we know may be helpful. How do we do it without sounding like we are giving advice or suggesting what the solution should be? One common way is to ask if it is OK to "offer" information or observations. "Would it be OK if I shared some information about relapse?" "I have had some experiences that are related to what you are struggling with. Would it be OK if I share those with you?" By asking, you are reminding the client that they are responsible for what happens, and giving them a choice about whether sharing information or experiences would help *their* task of solving their problem.

SIGN #3: THE CLIENT MAKES DECISIONS FROM THEIR PERSPECTIVE

A corollary to the rule that the client is always responsible is that 'clients must decide from their unique perspective'—their values, beliefs, and hopes.

If the counselor truly accepts this statement, then they must accept that their own advice has limited value. How can a counselor know what a client should do? Only clients truly know their own perspective—their own values and beliefs. Your job as a peer counselor is to help your client think the problem through **from their perspective**, so that they can make a good decision.

Here we can understand the value of empathy and listening. Genuine empathy will allow the counselor to better understand the internal perspective of the client. This is the raw material of the decisions that clients need to make. When the counselor listens well, they and the client will have a better understanding of the client's perspective—which will support the client making decisions. Indirectly, empathy and good listening communicate to the client that their perspective is important to solving the problem.

SIGN #4: THERE IS A CLEAR FOCUS AND GOAL FOR THE WORK

Healthcare is required to involve the explicit discussion of a goal or goals for any treatment. If you are working in an accredited hospital or healthcare organization, you are going to hear a great deal about treatment goals and treatment plans. The value of this approach is that both clients and providers know what they are trying to achieve, and any services being provided should make sense in light of the target goal. This is just as true for peer counseling as for any other intervention. You and your client will want to set a clear goal for your work: What does your client want to change?

I would suggest that you talk about this early in your work with any client and that you talk about that goal in almost every session. Be sure that the goal is stated by the client and it reflects their desires and expectations. You will want to document the goal in your clinical notes. I like to see the goal phrased in the client's words (e.g., "The goal of peer counseling is to increase the number of friendships I have so that I feel less lonely."). I also like to see the goal repeated in every clinical note. The stated goal serves a number of purposes, including:

1. **It Is the Target for the Work.** It is easy for clinical work to start to shift in focus. "Mission drift" can cause peer counseling to keep changing focus and eventually to achieve nothing. A clear goal that is stated in the documentation for each session, and talked about during the counseling at regular intervals, will help keep the work focused.

2. **It Provides a Marker for Change.** I often find that clients will either achieve one goal and then want to add a new goal, or will want to change the goal as they better understand what they want. The treatment goal should change as the client wants to change the focus of their peer counseling. This can be a clear indicator of the progress the client is making.

3. **It Tells Others About the Value of the Peer Counseling.** Every service that any client uses is designed to produce a benefit. Given the cost of healthcare and social services, there are always people who are looking to eliminate services that may not actually produce any benefit. By having a clear goal that the client wants to achieve, you are ensuring that anyone can see the value your peer counseling is providing.

SIGN #5: WE ASSUME THEY ARE AMBIVALENT AND HELP THEM SEE AND EXPLORE IT

Ambivalence is a common part of being human. Experienced peer counselors know that people are ambivalent about almost everything, and particularly about those things that are important to them. The ambivalence may be under the surface—we may not be aware of it at times—but it is there. Consider how you feel about your job. While you may love your job in some ways, and even be very committed to staying in that job, you likely dislike some things about it. We typically have mixed feelings about the most important parts of our lives: things we like, things we don't like, things we hope for, things we wish were different.

This is particularly true of areas of our lives that create problems for us—areas that we may want to talk to a peer counselor about. Let's use substance abuse as an example. I may be worried that I am drinking too much. I may enjoy drinking: the taste of alcohol, the feeling I get when I have been drinking, and the relief from my worries that I feel when I am drunk. At the same time, I may hate the feeling of being hungover, may worry about the damage I see it doing to my marriage, and may fear what it is doing to my body.

For peer counseling to be effective, people need to review and recognize that they have ambivalent feelings and to see those feelings as part of solving the problem they are focusing on. Clients often don't feel that this is OK. They may not feel like they can or should have mixed feelings about something: "I should not like to drink." "I should not talk badly about my marriage." "I should not be so afraid of getting better." By assuming ambivalence, the peer counselor encourages clients to better explore the full range of what they feel. The more the client recognizes and includes the full range of their feelings in the discussion, the more likely that they will make a decision that will turn into real action.

SIGN #6: PEER COUNSELING INCLUDES BOTH PROBLEM-SOLVING AND SUPPORT

While most peer counseling situations will focus on a problem, and thus on solving that problem, the effective peer counselor knows that simply being supportive of the person is often half the battle.

In many cases, when the peer counselor is truly empathic, congruent, and communicates respect and unconditional positive regard, the client will start to change. The support the peer counselor gives leads the client to be more aware of their own thoughts and feelings—more accepting of their own experiences. This leads them to think more clearly about the problem, which allows them to make better decisions.

In contrast, peer counselors who try to help clients solve problems but who are not supportive (providing empathy, congruence, respect, and positive regard) often find the problem-solving to be ineffective. Without true support, clients typically don't feel comfortable thinking about the problem in a truly open way, and so don't come up with lasting solutions.

Unfortunately, peer counselors, particularly new peer counselors, feel tempted to emphasize the problem-solving aspect of their peer counseling, and are less attentive to the support. Counselors often feel some urgency to help the client solve their problem— to help them relieve the pain associated with the problem. Counselors, like many clients, are often just impatient—they want to solve the problem now, and they often feel that problem-solving is clearer and easier to understand. Counselors can also feel insecure about their own skills, and so emphasize problem-solving too much in order to make sure the peer counseling is a success. Unfortunately, problem-solving without genuine support is often a losing formula—it is not effective in the long run. Patience and a tenacious focus on providing genuine support as part of problem-solving will be more successful when it comes to getting to a lasting solution.

SIGN #7: THE PEER COUNSELOR'S CARING AND RESPECT ARE GENUINE AND EVIDENT IN LARGE AND SMALL THINGS

We are all good at reading the agendas of other people.

Researchers suggest that children as young as twelve months old start trying to figure out the agendas of other people and using that information to guide their own behavior. By the time those children grow to adulthood, they are very good at identifying other people's underlying agendas, even when they are hidden (Rakoczy, 2022).

Your clients will almost all have good skills at identifying genuine caring, empathy, and trustworthiness. I often feel that the primary agenda of my new clients during the first meeting I have with them is to determine whether I actually have these qualities, particularly whether I actually care about them. Your clients will likely do the same. Given their ability to identify agendas in you and others, you want to consider the following:

1. **Review Your Own Motives for Providing Peer Counseling.** Among your motives, is there genuine concern and respect for the people you will serve? If that is not present your clients are likely to see past any efforts to pretend.

2. **Consider How Consistently You Show These Qualities to Your Clients.** If your caring and respect are genuine, they should be consistently evident in the things you say and do. They should also be consistent over time. Your clients will be looking for times when your actions are not consistent, and will draw conclusions about you based on those.

3. **Review What You Communicate in Large and Small Behaviors.** Researchers have been discovering how clients and others observe small behaviors as evidence of how other people really feel. These behaviors are called *microaffirmations*, defined as "small acts, which are often

ephemeral, hard-to-see, events that are public and private, often unconscious . . . which occur wherever people wish to help others to succeed" (Rowe, 2008).

Researchers have found that these small behaviors are being read constantly by clients with important consequences for the treatment (Topor, Bøe & Larsen, 2018). The behaviors fall into a few categories, including the following:

- **Words.** Small things that we say. Do we call them by name? Do we talk as though we respect them? Do we talk in a way that suggests they are people just like us, or do we act like they have a lower status as someone who is in treatment?

- **Gestures.** Body language and facial expressions are often seen as more genuine than our words. Do we have good eye contact? Do we sit in a way that suggests genuine interest? Does our facial expression reflect genuine understanding of what they are saying and that we care about them?

- **Actions.** These include small behaviors on our part that reflect genuine concern over and above simply doing a job. Examples include trying to adjust times of meetings based on the client's needs, chitchatting at times in a way that communicates respect for the client as another person with a life like ours, and being responsive in a timely way, which clients interpret as the peer counselor feeling that the client's needs are important.

Some of these microaffirmations are simply things we do when we genuinely care for and respect our clients. Others we can actually practice to ensure we are showing our clients the caring and respect we have for them. In a study of grade school students, teachers were assigned to either greet their students each morning in any way they usually do or to greet each student individually at the door of the classroom as they entered for the first time each morning. The greeting had to include their name, good eye contact, and a simple comment suggesting recognition of them as a person or a positive feeling about them coming. "I like your new shoes." "I'm glad you're here today." When the teachers gave the careful greetings, students performed better and worked harder at their schoolwork—just by being met in a caring way each morning (Allday & Pakurar, 2007).

We want to develop habits that consistently communicate our caring and respect for our clients. Don't assume that because you feel those things for your clients that they can see it. They are looking for small and large evidence that you care, and so it is worthwhile developing large and small habits that show it.

CHAPTER 4

COMMON MISTAKES

It is helpful to keep an eye out for common mistakes that peer counselors, particularly new peer counselors, often fall into. These typically happen without the peer counselor recognizing it, and despite the best intentions and the best training. Counselors who keep a watchful eye on their own behavior will pick up on these mistakes and can then correct them in order to improve their peer counseling.

MISTAKE #1: TALKING TOO MUCH

In general, the majority of any effective peer counseling session should be spent with the client talking and the peer counselor listening. Many new or poorly trained peer counselors spend too much time talking and not enough time listening. There are a few common reasons for this:

- The peer counselor is anxious about counseling and fills the session by talking as an expression of their anxiety or as a means of controlling the situation.

- The peer counselor is uncomfortable with silence and so talks as a way to avoid any silences in the session.

- The peer counselor feels that they have the solutions for the client, and if the client simply hears all the wisdom that the peer counselor has, their problems will be solved.

- The peer counselor enjoys the attention they receive when they are talking and may feel wise or important. They consciously or unconsciously are using the client as an audience.

Regardless of the cause, talking too much and listening too little is a losing strategy for peer counseling. Imagine that an invisible scientist is sitting in on every peer counseling session you have, counting the number of sentences you are speaking and the number of sentences your client is speaking. If your number is as large or larger than your client's, the scientist holds up a big red flag. On average you should be talking about a third of the time. When it is consistently more than 50 percent, you should consult with your supervisor about what you are doing and how to improve.

Clients need to talk. They need to provide information about the problem, talk about how to change, and feel supported and understood. They need to hear themselves talking about these things if they are going to change them. None of these things happen when the peer counselor talks most of the time.

MISTAKE #2: INTERROGATING

As we will see, questions are an important tool for the peer counselor. When the peer counselor asks too many questions, many clients start to feel that the conversation is about the peer counselor and not about them. Counselors who ask too many questions typically do so for a few common reasons:

- They like talking or controlling the meeting too much. Interrogating can reflect that the peer counselor is feeling anxious or feels a need to fill the silence or take control of the conversation.

- Too many questions can also reflect the mistaken view by the peer counselor that they will be able to solve the client's problem themselves. "If I can just figure this all out, my client's problem will be solved." They ask many questions, hoping to uncover the solution for the client. Unfortunately, they have forgotten that it is what the client thinks that is most important—not what the peer counselor thinks.

MISTAKE #3: CONFUSING YOUR VIEW AND THE CLIENT'S VIEW

A related mistake occurs when the peer counselor confuses their view of the problem/solution with the view of the client. Because you are two separate people, you will each have different views, and what you value and what you would like to see for a resolution will differ. Since it is their problem, and they must be the person who solves that problem, it is their perspective that is most important. Using empathy, you gain a good understanding of their perspective and help them use that perspective to solve their problem.

When peer counselors confuse their values, preferences, and understanding with those of the client, the peer counseling process gets confused and bogs down. The client starts to feel misunderstood and frustrated. The peer counselor feels frustrated because they feel they have figured out the solution but the client is not changing. The solutions that arise typically don't work well because they do not fully reflect what the client thinks and wants.

MISTAKE #4: ACTING AS THOUGH YOU ARE RESPONSIBLE

Counselors don't usually say this to their clients directly but may convey it indirectly in many different ways. Below are a few examples:

- Telling the client how to solve their problem.

- Talking to the client in a way that suggests the peer counselor knows or will figure out the right solution.

- Taking steps to solve the problem without the client's input.

- Taking steps to solve the problem when the client could take those steps.

- Taking steps to solve the problem in a way that suggests the peer counselor is "taking care of the client."

It is tempting for peer counselors to start to feel and act as though they are responsible. It may make them feel important or wise. It may give the peer counselor a sense of control, particularly when the client's life feels out of control. It may feel more efficient than waiting for the client to take responsibility for their problems. It may feel like the generous or caring thing to do—to "help" the client out by solving the problem.

Despite all these tempting reasons to take responsibility for solving the client's problem, this strategy will almost always lead to failure. By taking responsibility, you are indirectly telling your client that they don't have to be responsible, or are not capable of it. You also are undermining their need to be responsible for their own lives and problems. While clients in distress may feel relieved that someone is taking control of the problem for them, over time they will resent what you have done and the relationship will break down.

As we've mentioned in the prior chapter, effective peer counselors are tenacious in holding the client responsible for the peer counseling and for solving the problem.

MISTAKE #5: JUDGING THE OTHER PERSON

If we truly accept that each person's experience is different and that they are responsible for their own decisions, we should come to a place where we are not judgmental about what our clients are doing. They are the ones who have to decide and the only ones who have the full knowledge to do so. It does no good for us to judge them. Unfortunately, they can usually tell when we are being judgmental—even if we try to hide it. What do you feel when you can tell someone else is judging you? Most people feel a need to pull back and be defensive. By allowing yourself to be judgmental, you are putting your trust and, thus, your peer counseling relationship at risk. When I have talked to clients who report that their peer counselor is acting in a judgmental way, I encourage the client to speak openly about it with the counselor. If the client finds out that the peer counselor does think poorly of them because of something they've done or something they are, I encourage clients to end the relationship. We do no one any good by being judgmental.

So why do peer counselors do it? There are a few common reasons:

- Some people tend to evaluate everything. Evaluating things and looking for problems comes very easily to them and so they do this very naturally. It can be quite useful for some jobs, such as quality inspector or editor. It is not good for peer counseling. If you recognize that trait in yourself, I would suggest you talk with your supervisor.

- Peer counselors may judge their clients as an expression of their own anger that the client is not doing what the peer counselor thinks they should do. This may reflect the bad decisions of the client, but it also reflects the failure of the peer counselor to maintain the clear belief that the client is always responsible for their decisions.

- Peer counselors may be tempted to judge their clients when they are feeling insecure or anxious about how they, the peer counselor, are doing in their own job. Particularly early-career peer counselors may feel that their clients' choices reflect on their own skill as a counselor. "If my client makes bad decisions, then I must be a bad counselor!" The real problem is feeling insecure about your skills and not the client's behavior. More experienced peer counselors know that some of their clients will make bad decisions and that this does not mean they are doing a bad counseling job.

MISTAKE #7: BEING IMPATIENT

With more experience, I've become convinced that patience and persistence are the most important virtues in life. The patient and persistent person is almost always successful. That is true when we are working on things that we are responsible for. It is even more important when we are working with other people and we are not responsible for their behavior.

Solving problems and making changes takes time. Recovery almost always takes a great deal of time and has ups and downs. You want to cultivate patience and persistence at the very core of your work as a peer counselor. In most peer counseling relationships, there comes a time when the client wonders if the peer counselor will give up on them. Usually this is because the client is wondering if they will give up on themselves. By holding the hope for our clients in a patient and persistent way, we make it possible for them to persevere.

MISTAKE #8: NOT FOLLOWING THROUGH

The client has to do the heavy lifting in the peer counseling process—but what you *are* responsible for is very important. When you drop the ball and fail to do something you agreed to do for the client, this is a big deal. It is important that you see it as a big deal and that you let the client know that you see it as such. They will see not keeping your word as a potential indicator that you don't care or don't believe in their success, so follow through whenever possible, and apologize when it's not.

MISTAKE #9: ACTING LIKE A PSYCHOTHERAPIST (OR ANY OTHER TYPE OF PROVIDER THAT YOU ARE NOT)

Peer counseling is a powerful tool, particularly when combined with other professional providers and other powerful tools such as medication, psychotherapy, rehabilitation, and peer support groups. The key to any clinical treatment is to have collaborative help by talented professionals who are well trained in providing the tools they are supposed to provide. As mentioned earlier, it is not in your client's interest or your own to start providing services that you are not trained for. The largest temptation may be to start doing "psychotherapy," but I have known other peer counselors who start to give advice on medications and other services.

MISTAKE #10: TAKING YOUR EYE OFF THE BALL

Healthcare and social service settings tend to be very busy places to work. There are a lot of demands and often some confusion. You are likely to have a number of clients, each with different needs. Some will be in crisis. Others will have unusual needs that will require special attention.

Your clients will know that you are busy, but they will still want to know that you care about them and that your work with them is as important to you as it is to them. Good peer counselors keep a keen focus on the interests of their clients. It is by far the most important thing that you will do in your work as a peer counselor. Your work puts you in a very privileged position in the lives of people who are in a very vulnerable spot. You need to always act in a way that demonstrates awareness of that very important place and that you know you can hurt your clients if you are not careful.

Don't let the competing work demands cause you to take your eye off the ball. Your client's recovery is the key to everything you are doing. All other concerns or tasks are secondary to that. If you forget the guiding goal for everything, your work will have little or no impact. Some of the most common distractions include:

- The demands of a busy workday.

- The number of clients competing for your time and attention. This is particularly true when organizations are not careful about caseload sizes. Research shows a direct relationship between the number of people we serve and how much impact our work has. Don't get caught in an impossible job, assigned so many clients that you can't help anyone.

- Bureaucratic demands such as documentation and compliance with agency procedures. Documentation and agency guidelines have an important role. But they are not the reason you are providing peer counseling. I've seen peer counselors who, over time, get confused and start to act as though the most important priority is getting all their paperwork done. The welfare of the client is priority number one, and everything else truly makes sense only when we remember that priority.

- Your own agendas in your work. We all want to have a job that we enjoy and where we are seen as doing good work. I have seen peer counselors (and other healthcare professionals) slowly starting to prioritize their own comfort (a nice office, comfortable hours, etc.) over their work with their clients. I've seen others start to act like their own professional ambitions are more important than their clients. A good job will include elements that address your comfort and your professional ambitions, but comfort and ambition should never be the top priority in the helping professions.

Take some time to complete the self-evaluation in the following exercise. Your ratings should help you identify some areas of vulnerability for your work. Use your overall ratings to again identify two areas for improvement and set goals for how you will accomplish that improvement.

EXERCISE 2: SELF-EVALUATION

Rate yourself below, indicating how often these common problems are present in your peer counseling sessions.

I am talking too much.
1   2   3   4   5   6   7   8   9   10
Never   Sometimes   Always

I am interrogating my client.
1   2   3   4   5   6   7   8   9   10
Never   Sometimes   Always

I confuse my views and their views.
1   2   3   4   5   6   7   8   9   10
Never   Sometimes   Always

I act as though I am responsible for my client's behavior.
1   2   3   4   5   6   7   8   9   10
Never   Sometimes   Always

I am judgmental toward my client.
1   2   3   4   5   6   7   8   9   10
Never   Sometimes   Always

I am impatient with my client.
1   2   3   4   5   6   7   8   9   10
Never   Sometimes   Always

I fail to follow through with something I said I would do.
1   2   3   4   5   6   7   8   9   10
Never   Sometimes   Always

I act like a psychotherapist instead of peer counselor.
1   2   3   4   5   6   7   8   9   10
Never   Sometimes   Always

I lose track of the overall goal of the client's recovery.
1   2   3   4   5   6   7   8   9   10
Never   Sometimes   Always

Plan for further development: Choose one or two items above that you want to improve on. Set a goal and plan below for each.

Goal 1: To reduce the common mistake of

____

Plan:

Goal 2: To reduce the common mistake of

____

Plan:

CHAPTER 5

WHAT THE CLIENT BRINGS TO THE SITUATION

Each peer counseling situation involves a number of elements. You want to become very adept at recognizing those elements quickly, as your ability to do so will determine how helpful you can be.

The client brings the most important elements to the situation. Research has shown that the outcome of psychotherapy is dependent more on the client and what they bring to the situation than the therapist. It seems very likely that this is also true of peer counseling. So, what does the client bring?

THE PROBLEM

The client brings the problem (or problems) that will serve as the focus of the peer counseling. Helping the client solve that problem is the goal of your work. Unfortunately, there are a few challenges in understanding the problem:

1. The client may not fully understand the problem, or may think it is different than what it really is. A client may want to "be more accepting of my partner" when they actually are very angry and don't want to face their own anger. They may say the problem is their boss's being critical when it is really that they don't like their job and don't perform at even a minimal level.

2. The client may not be able to articulate the problem. They know it is there, but it is very difficult for them to put it into words. For example, the client may say they feel "depressed." They do have symptoms of depression, but these might be closely related to a stressor at work they can't really recognize at this point.

3. The client has multiple problems, more than what they understood when they started, which may cause them to feel overwhelmed, or simply confused.

THEIR PERSON

The problem (and the solution) will only make sense in the context of who the client is. What do they care about? What do they value? What are their strengths and talents? How do their background experiences and personality relate to the problem and to the peer counseling? You have to get to know them if you are to understand the real problem and get to a real solution.

THEIR GOALS AND EXPECTATIONS

The problem, and the peer counseling, can be framed only by what the client wants to see change. Clients with the same "problem" can have very different goals for solving that problem. Some clients are very clear on what their goal is. Others are not at all clear, and so the peer counseling has to include identifying the goal and then pursuing it.

CLUES

Peer counseling can be similar to detective work. You and your client are trying to figure out how the problem came about and how to solve it. To do so, you may need clues that only the client can provide. These may be background characteristics or experiences in their past. They may be patterns in how they have behaved or been treated in the past. They may be patterns in how they think of the world or themselves. Your job is to work with your client to identify and understand the clues they bring and then help your client use them to find a way to accomplish the goal they have set.

THEIR SOCIAL NETWORK: FAMILY AND FRIENDS

No client can be understood without understanding those around them. We all are connected to others, and those individuals have a major influence on us. Family and friends, and even casual acquaintances, have a big impact on how we think and feel about life and ourselves. Problems are often caused and/or solved with the influence of others. You should always be listening to identify and understand the client's social network and the social connections that were important in their past.

THEIR AWARENESS AND BLIND SPOTS

The famous psychiatrist Carl Jung said the goal of all of life is become more and more aware of ourselves and our experience. This means that we are not aware of much of our experience. We all have blind spots that limit how we live. The problem is that blind spots produce gaps in our knowledge, and gaps in our knowledge create problems. Always listen for what your clients are aware of and note what their blind spots are.

CHAPTER 6

WHAT YOU BRING TO THE SITUATION

Researchers studying psychotherapy suggest that, after the client, the most influential factor in the psychotherapy setting is the therapist. Again, it seems very likely that this is also true for peer counseling. So, what do you bring to the counseling situation?

A LISTENING EAR, CARING, INTEREST

As we've already talked about, good peer counselors are good listeners. Listening is direct evidence of caring about and interest in the client and their problem. That is what they are really looking for and so the ability to listen well, and to show caring and interest, is absolutely critical if the peer counseling is to have any impact.

A SEPARATE PERSPECTIVE

In most peer counseling situations, if the client could have solved their problem by themselves already, they would have. That is why they are approaching you for help—they have tried and not been able to solve the problem alone. You provide a second set of eyes on the situation and offer your different perspective to the client. Life is complex, and most significant problems require the input of multiple people. In many situations, teams of people are much more successful than individuals because when different people view the same problem, they come up with a range of possible solutions. Peer counseling brings that new perspective to the client to help them find solutions they may not have considered before.

YOUR EXPERIENCE

As a Peer Support Specialist, you will bring your personal experience with illness and recovery to the situation. As a peer counselor, you'll gain additional experience as you work with many clients and have many different peer counseling conversations. Those experiences will create patterns and examples that will guide your work as you go forward. This happens somewhat automatically, as your brain simply starts to figure out the most likely patterns associated with this type of work. You can help it happen more quickly by continuing to pursue more education and training in peer counseling, and by working with experienced supervisors who can point out key patterns in your work.

YOUR INSIGHTS

Every person has developed a number of insights that they find helpful in solving life's problems. They may be big generalities or small life lessons. You bring your own lessons and insights, based on your own life and on your work as a Peer Support Specialist. While your insights are not guaranteed to help your clients, there is a good chance that they will.

YOUR VALUES

Different people value different things. Your clients will be watching for what you value, and your values will influence them. We've already talked about how the value and respect you show for your client will have a big influence on the peer counseling. Other things that you value, and the things you don't value, will also likely influence your clients. Your value for recovery, for example, will be a big influence. Your role in providing peer support, too, points to a core value of helping others and generosity. Be thoughtful about your values and how they can be used to better help your clients.

YOUR BIASES AND BLIND SPOTS

You will also, undoubtedly, bring your own biases and blind spots. We all have these, and there is no escaping the reality that they come into the peer counseling conversation and have an impact on your clients. This is the reason I am always motivated to grow in my ability to recognize and correct more of my blind spots. The benefits are not just for me but for my clients.

CHAPTER 7

LISTENING

At the core of effective peer counseling is good listening.

It is not giving good advice. People often don't want advice and/or don't actually listen to it.

It is not being able to recognize what the client's problem is. You may be a wonderfully perceptive peer counselor, but your insight does not necessarily translate into the client agreeing or doing anything with your insight.

Effective listening is your most powerful tool, because it is what leads people to change their thinking and thus their behavior.

Listening seems so simple. We do it all the time, but do we do it well? I would say typically we don't. We listen to others every day, but most of the time our listening is of fairly poor quality. We listen for important things—often, for things that are relevant to us. But we underestimate how challenging it is to really listen to others, and so we miss opportunities to fully support them.

I have trained many peer counselors over my career. The most challenging lesson for them to learn is to recognize the full power and importance of good listening.

BEING INTERESTED

I find people to be very complex and endlessly interesting. Each person's experience is different, and how they interpret their experience is different as well. As a peer counselor, you get a chance to hear about people's world from a very privileged position. It is a great honor to have people share their internal world with you. Build on your appreciation for that experience. Your clients will be able to see your interest and care by the way you approach this work.

BASIC WAYS OF SHOWING RESPECTFUL INTEREST

Consider the following indirect ways of showing respect:

Posture: Try to get in a habit of using your body language to communicate that you are fully focused on your client, for example:
(1) Have an open posture. Crossing of legs and folding of arms is generally seen as a guarded or tense stance. Some of us have the habit of doing this, but try to avoid it as much as possible and see if you can get comfortable. (2) Lean a little toward your client. This posture tends to communicate interest. We often lean away from people when we want a little distance. When we lean too far in, we typically create tension by intruding on others' personal space.

Eye Contact: "The eyes are the window to the soul" is a useful reminder. You can see a lot in the eyes of your clients, but they can also see a lot in yours. You want to maintain good eye contact, as this expresses your interest in them. Too little eye contact communicates disinterest, but staring at your client is likely to make them uncomfortable, so striking the right balance is important.

Facial Expression: Be aware of what you are communicating with your facial expressions. Your goal is to communicate caring and interest. When clients are talking about topics that can be challenging to hear, you want to check in with your face—what are you expressing? I find my face can let me know when I am uncomfortable, even when I don't realize that I am. Work hard to keep an open, supportive expression, and your client will often continue to talk to you.

Clothing and Personal Space: Your client will draw conclusions about you based on your clothing. If you dress very formally, they will feel more formal, which may be helpful or not. If you are too casual, they are likely to feel that this is a sign of disrespect either to them or to your work. Clothing is often relative, and so you will want to see what other people in your role in your organization and in your area are wearing and ensure you are thoughtful about what you wear and what you want to say with it.

We all have preferences for personal space. If people stand too close to us, or touch us in ways that feel inappropriate, we all tend to get uncomfortable and feel a need to pull away. If people stand far away, we also draw conclusions about that   typically interpreting it as an indication of disinterest. Look for the right distance and be attentive to how your clients react to it. Be particularly careful about touching clients, such as hugging them or putting a hand on their shoulder. You may feel that this is OK (e.g., "I'm just a hugger"), but the key question is what your client thinks about it. Too much touching by peer counselors can quickly kill peer counseling relationships before they even start. I would encourage you to be conservative until you are clear on the experiences and preferences of your client.

How You Talk—the Tone of Your Voice, Volume, Speed, and Emphasis: I used to have an office next to a colleague who had a fairly loud voice. The wall was thin enough that I could hear her comments to her clients, but I could not understand the words. I was amazed at how much I could read about her feelings based simply on the tone of her voice and the speed at which she talked. I heard when she was tense, anxious, bored, or angry. That means your clients can and are doing the same about you. Be alert to the way you talk, not just your words.

LOOKING FOR THOUGHTS, FEELINGS, AND ACTIONS

People are complex, and what they say is often complex. One way to organize your efforts to listen involves tracking three key domains: thoughts, feelings, and actions.

When a client says, "I feel really down today," they are talking only about one of the domains—feelings. When they say, "I think this job is not right for me," they are talking only about a thought. When they say, "I didn't show up for my doctor's appointment," they are talking only about actions.

Most of the time people are going to mention all three as they talk with you. For example, a client may tell you, "I am so mad at my boss today. He went over my head to get someone else to take a project that was mine. I told him off, which was probably not a good idea, but at this point, I don't care."

If we pull this apart, we can identify:
1. Feelings: I am angry, and I don't care that I may have hurt myself by how I acted.

2. Actions: I told my boss off.
3. Thoughts: I think he acted unfairly. I think I may get a negative reaction to my behavior.

All three of the domains may be key to helping your client understand themselves better and change their behavior. It could be that for this client, it is the feeling that is most important, but you will know by the context and the client whether feelings, actions, or thoughts are most important. At this point, you just want to be sure you are hearing and tracking all three.

Feelings: The person may say what they are feeling (e.g., "I'm angry"), but often, they say it indirectly ("That seems quite unfair!"), or only in their tone of voice or posture. You will want to always track what your clients are feeling as they talk with you.

Actions: What are they telling you about what they did or did not do? What actions of others are they telling you about? Actions are key to helping understand and change situations.

Thoughts: Again, the client may say this directly or indirectly. You may need to ask yourself, "What were they thinking about this situation that led them to react that way?"

You want to build your ability to accurately recognize and track these three domains as you listen to your clients. At the end of the chapter are some exercises to help you identify the domains. You can write down what you hear, and then check it with the answers in Appendix B. Don't be surprised if your answers don't match those in the appendix exactly. There is some variation in every instance of listening—some wiggle room that may reflect different but valid interpretations. When your answers are significantly different, you'll want to review those situations to ensure you understand why you heard it so differently.

WHY IS LISTENING SO POWERFUL?

Listening appears to be a passive activity. On the surface it does not appear as influential as trying to push or actively persuade your client to change their behavior. How can it be "powerful"?

First of all, we need to agree that trying to push people to do things they don't want to do is not really powerful and not particularly helpful. We all tend to resent when people try to push us to do something. We all have ways of not doing what we are pushed to do, whether it is actively or passively resisting. Even small children have already learned skills for resisting pressure from their parents. Pressuring others is not powerful.

The power of listening comes from several key factors:

1. By focusing on listening, you encourage the client to take the talking role. This seems simple and obvious, but it is critical. Virtually no one changes by being told what they should do. Real change has to involve the person talking.

2. Listening is called a "nondirective" activity. You are not overtly "setting the direction" for the conversation. By not setting the direction, however, you are forcing the client to do so and to take charge of what is talked about. Since the goal of the conversation is to discuss what they want to change, you are forcing them to define the problem and the change they want. Clients often have taken a passive or avoidant stance toward the problem, or have become so discouraged that they've stopped trying to solve it. You are forcing them to step back into the role of solving their own problem.

3. By listening, you are clearly communicating that the solution to the problem lies inside the client: in their feelings and thoughts, their past and present experiences, and in their decisions. Most clients don't understand

some key aspect of their own experience and may not want to see something about themselves that is creating the problem. Listening is a forceful way to continue to redirect them back to themselves, both as a source of important information and as the key decider. Some clients so uncomfortable with their own feelings and thoughts that they try to fill the peer counseling session with conversation about sports and weather. They would love to have a peer counselor who would fill the session by talking about their own thoughts. By listening, the effective peer counselor keeps the client focused on what is important.

4. Good peer counselors don't just listen and reflect back everything that the client says. Instead, they listen to everything but reflect back only the parts that seem most important. In that way, the peer counselor helps the client focus on what appears to be most important. I always see this as "selective listening." We hear everything, but we are listening most attentively for the patterns related to the problem and the client's goal. This subtle direction is difficult for most clients to resist. They hear you reflect what they are saying, and they follow that into a deeper discussion. Again, what looks like a nondirective activity actually involves a lot of subtle direction.

Try the following exercise to help you develop your ability to recognize and track thoughts, feelings, and actions.

EXERCISE 3: LISTENING FOR THOUGHTS, FEELINGS, AND ACTIONS

For each of the following statements from a hypothetical client, write down what you are hearing in each of the three categories. Try to get all the content they are sharing without adding more than what they are actually saying.

1. "I'm really glad you are willing to talk with me. I asked my doctor to refer me to a peer counselor, but they just ignored me. It makes me so mad that they don't pay any attention to what I want. I don't really even talk to them any more—I just skip most of my appointments. If they are not going to listen to me, why should I listen to them?"

What do you hear about their thoughts?

What do you hear about their feelings?

What do you hear about their actions?

2. "Are you a peer counselor? My psychologist said I was supposed to meet with you, but they didn't say why. I guess they thought I needed more help than I was getting. They didn't say it, but I think I'm getting more and more depressed. They are probably worried that I'll do something stupid."

What do you hear about their thoughts?

What do you hear about their feelings?

What do you hear about their actions?

3. "I went to my first AA meeting last night—it was actually pretty good! I met a very nice person who was also there for the first time—they were VERY nice. We sat together during the meeting and hung out afterward. I think I could fit into that group. I didn't say anything in the meeting, but I liked what I heard. I plan to go again next week."

What do you hear about their thoughts?

What do you hear about their feelings?

What do you hear about their actions?

CHAPTER 8

REFLECTING

Client: *"I'm really mad at my mother today because she won't lend me one hundred dollars."*

Peer Counselor: *"You are really mad at your mother today because she won't lend you one hundred dollars."*

I have heard jokes from clients about how counselors reflect back their comments like the quotes above. It is a good example of bad reflecting—something a parrot could do. Let's talk about good reflecting.

Just because you are a good listener and can very accurately hear what your client is saying doesn't mean that this is helpful to your client. How do they know you heard and understand them? This is where reflecting comes in. Reflecting is a type of comment you make while you are listening. Like a mirror, a reflecting statement shows the client something about what they've just said.

THE GOALS OF REFLECTING

Reflecting has a number of key goals, including:

1. **Letting the Client Know You Are Listening.** An accurate reflection proves that you understand what they said.

2. **Creating an Opportunity for You to Check to See If You Heard Them Accurately.** If you misheard them, they can easily correct you. Client corrections happen all the time, and are very helpful.

3. **Letting the Client Hear What They Are Saying.** Often clients don't even realize what they are feeling or thinking until they hear themselves say it out loud or hear it reflected back to them. You are telling them what they are saying so that they can really hear themselves.

4. **Directing the Client's Attention to a Key Part of What They Said.** The most important part of their statement may be the thoughts they are having. It may be the feelings they are experiencing. It may be the actions they were describing. You may want to reflect what you think is most important in order to direct their attention to that element.

THE STRUCTURE OF REFLECTING

Good peer counselors routinely use reflecting statements in peer counseling. They don't just do this in the first conversation, but throughout. It's not necessary to reflect the client's comments after every sentence—that would interrupt the client too much. Do it when it seems natural in the flow of the conversation. Simply repeating what the client said, like a parrot, communicates disrespect and annoys most clients. Instead, paraphrase what the client has been saying and offer it as an opportunity for the client to hear what the peer counselor thinks they understand. For example, say your client tells you, "My doctor is kind of a jerk. He acts like I should do whatever he says and gets annoyed if I don't agree with him!" Here are some examples of good reflections on that statement.

General Reflecting Statements:
- "Sounds like your doctor acts like you have to listen to him. He's not open to hearing your views."
- "Sounds like you feel your doctor is not very good. He just does what he wants without listening."

Reflecting Feelings:
- "Your doctor makes you feel angry and disrespected."
- "He makes you feel frustrated. He doesn't seem to want to listen."
- "Your doctor irritates you sometimes. He doesn't seem interested in your views."

Reflecting Thoughts:
- "Your doctor acts like you should just follow his instructions."
- "You think your doctor wants you to be quiet and follow his directions."

Reflecting Actions:
- "When you disagree with him, he doesn't want to hear it."
- "He doesn't respond well when you state your views and desires."
- "You don't sit quietly and follow everything he says, and it irritates him."

EXERCISE 4: REFLECTIONS

For each of the following statements from a hypothetical client, write at least one possible reflection for each of the four categories (simple, feelings, thoughts, actions). Some possible answers are found in Appendix B.

1. "I've got to go to court tomorrow for a DUI. I'm not sure what is going to happen—I've never done this before. Could be really bad."

Simple reflection:

Reflecting the feelings:

Reflecting the thoughts:

Reflecting the actions:

2. "My nurse said I'm not losing weight fast enough. I don't think they believe me that I'm doing all of the exercises, but I am! Losing weight has always been really hard for me—you'd think they would understand that."

Simple reflection:

Reflecting the feelings:

Reflecting the thoughts:

Reflecting the actions:

3. "My doctor referred me to this cancer support group at the hospital. I went and there were only four people there and they were all really old. They looked really sick too—I'm not that sick! It was depressing! I can't relate to them—what a waste of my time."

Simple reflection:

Reflecting the feelings:

Reflecting the thoughts:

Reflecting the actions:

PACING

Your goal is to be alongside your client during these conversations. Picture it like joining someone who is walking down the street. If you walk at a pace that matches theirs, you'll stay right with them. If you move too fast or too slow, you will get ahead or behind them, which typically creates strains in the conversation. Reflecting statements tell your client where you are with respect to them.

When you achieve the right pace to match the needs of your client, they will typically continue to talk and explore their thoughts and feelings. They don't have to wonder where you are going, because your reflections tell them you are right with them. Ideally, you are just there and they freely explore their thoughts and feelings. Your presence simply allows them to do that.

If you are moving too slow, your client will often appear bored or frustrated. The conversation is not tracking with what they want to talk about—it is going too slow.

If you are moving too fast, your client will often look confused or frustrated. They are not understanding why you are saying what you are saying. They may feel like you are taking the conversation somewhere they don't feel like going.

If you are not listening well, and your reflections show that what you hear is not what they are saying, they will again look frustrated. If you are not hearing them, they will not keep talking.

THE RISK OF SOUNDING FORMULAIC

People learning peer counseling skills are often concerned that they will sound fake or stilted when they reflect comments back. As we've seen, if you parrot back their comments exactly, clients will get irritated. If, however, you reflect back fairly accurate understandings in a way that shows that you are listening, the conversations will become more and more helpful.

CHAPTER 9

SUMMARIZING

At times you will need to summarize what your client has shared over a longer portion of the conversation. They will give you a lot of information, and so it can be useful, and even necessary, to help them organize those details into a simpler and more concise picture.

THE GOALS OF A GOOD SUMMARY STATEMENT

You can't reflect everything a client has said, but a brief summary includes all the key elements. A good summary should move the conversation forward in three ways:

1. **It Organizes a Larger Set of Disorganized Comments.** In this type of summary statement, you are creating some organization that is not apparent in what the client said. Thoughts and feelings are often disorganized when they are first expressed. Simply providing some organization in a summary often helps clients think more clearly about what they've said. If

you've gotten the organization wrong, your client will typically look confused.

2. **It Can Be a Foundation for the Next Part of the Discussion.** A good summary can function as a transition point in the discussion. It creates some impression that it is now time to talk about the next step. These types of summaries often end with a question (e.g., "Where do you think this is going?" or "What do you think is the next step now that we have that clear?").

3. **It Provides Some New Insight into a Confusing Situation.** In this type of summary, you are making a connection or drawing a conclusion about what the person is saying, but one that the person has not yet made themselves. You typically want to insert only things that you feel are very likely to be true and that your client is ready to see. If you are not correct or they are not ready to accept the insight, they will usually look confused or frustrated and you will need to backtrack.

PACING

A good summary statement will either summarize where the client is or provide a summary that is just ahead of where they are. If the summary is not keeping up with the client's comments—it is too simple or does not include what they have just talked about—they will look frustrated because it is not accurate.

If the summary is too far ahead of the client—it is too different from what they feel or you inserted an insight that they don't agree with or are not ready to accept—they will look confused because they don't understand the way you've summarized the discussion.

EXERCISE 5: SUMMARIZING

For each of the following statements from a hypothetical client, write a summary statement. Remember that good summary statements are usually shorter than the client's comments but organize those comments in a useful way.

1. "My medications are making me sleep better, which is something good. When I can't sleep at least six hours a night, I can't think clearly the next day and then I feel depressed. I've had three nights of good sleep in a row—that is the best in months! Maybe I could stop talking to the psychologist if I just got my sleep all settled. I don't like those talking sessions. They just make me feel tense afterward."
Write a possible summary statement for your client.
2. "My parents don't have much money and so I can't get the treatment I really need. I have no insurance and I haven't worked for a year. I can't imagine I can get over this anxiety without good treatment, but I can't afford it. I'm sure everyone else in this day treatment program here has good insurance. I bet I'm going to have to drop out."
Write a possible summary statement for your client.

3. "When my wife died, I lost everything. She was the center of my world. I had no friends. I couldn't stay in that house—it was too depressing. I moved here near my daughter in order to try to start over, but I don't know how to do that. I sit in my apartment all day alone—I can't stand it. I don't think my daughter understands what this is like. Maybe I should sign up for a dating app."

Write a possible summary statement for your client.

CHAPTER 10

ASKING GOOD QUESTIONS

Your clients are not going to tell you everything you will need to know to understand them, and so you are going to have to ask questions. Questions are designed to gather information—but they can do so much more!

Like reflections and summary statements, good questions show that you are listening. At times, clients can feel that questions disrupt the flow of the conversation or that you are asking questions because you are focused on your own interests instead of theirs. They may simply find the questions distracting from what they want to talk about. When there are too many questions, clients feel "interrogated" and the peer counseling starts to break down. Though a good question may add a new direction or emphasis, it keeps the client talking about what they are interested in and makes sense to them.

OPEN-ENDED VS. CLOSE-ENDED QUESTIONS

There are two types of questions. Close-ended questions seek specific information, and so the answers are usually limited and will tell you a limited amount about the client. These may be yes or no questions (e.g., "Do you want to apply for that job?") or questions with specific answers (e.g., "Which job do you want to apply for—the cooking or cleaning job?").

As a counselor, you want to become an expert in using open-ended questions. These questions don't call for a simple answer, and so you will typically get a lot more information about the person. For example, you could ask, "What are your thoughts about putting in a job application for these different jobs?" This type of question will usually lead your client to provide a range of information. What they choose to include is often very important, and tells you what is most salient to them. Such a question is an invitation to continue talking—to explore thoughts, feelings, and actions.

Here are some other ways to frame that same open-ended question.

1. "How are you thinking about your next steps for work?"

2. "I wonder how you are thinking about our last conversation about possible jobs you could apply for."

3. "What kinds of jobs would you be excited to apply for?"

4. "What do you think will work best for you if you do go after those jobs?"

THE NUMBER AND FREQUENCY OF QUESTIONS

Interrogation is a term we use for a one-sided conversation where one person asks a great deal of questions. People generally don't like to be interrogated. You will want to be careful about how many questions you ask and how frequently you ask them.

If you are doing a formal interview, your client will expect a lot of questions. For most peer counseling conversations, though, they will not. You can avoid asking too many questions by simply making more reflective and summary statements. When you do ask questions, it should be clear to your client why you are asking them, and they should hopefully think that it is part of your effort to help them. Here are some examples of open-ended questions that target different types of information.

QUESTIONS FOCUSING ON FACTS
1. "Tell me about your school history. Where did you go to school and how did that go?"
2. "What kinds of treatment have you tried in the past, and how did they work for you?"
3. "What has your sleep been like in the past few days, and how has that been for you?"

QUESTIONS FOCUSING ON FEELINGS AND REACTIONS
1. "Can you tell me more about that feeling?"
2. "How did that situation make you feel?"
3. "Can you tell me more about your reaction to that event?"
4. "So, you were irritated . . . were you feeling anything else?"
5. "I hear what they did—what were you feeling when they did that?"

QUESTIONS FOCUSING ON THOUGHTS AND IDEAS
1. "I hear you've been feeling down. What have you been thinking about while you've felt that way?"

2. "I wonder what kinds of thoughts you've been having in those situations."
3. "What did you anticipate was going to happen?"
4. "Is that a pattern in your thinking? How long have you noticed that? When do you notice it?"
5. "Do you have plans for dealing with that? Tell me about those."

QUESTIONS FOCUSING ON BEHAVIORS AND ACTIONS

1. "What did you do at that point?"
2. "What did your children do when you said that?"
3. "Are there things you tend to do when that happens?"
4. "What were you doing when your wife responded that way?"
5. "Have you noticed any pattern in your actions in those situations?"

PACING

Good questions either help the client talk more fully about the topic they want to discuss or lead them to talk about an important topic in a way that they understand.

If your question is not keeping up with the client's conversation, the client will look frustrated because the question is taking them away from what they want to say. They may also feel like you are not keeping up with them.

If your question is too far ahead of where they are going, they will often look confused. They don't know why you are asking that question and don't see how it is related to the discussion. You might be on target, but you'll want to back up a bit so that you stay with them.

CHAPTER 11

SELF-DISCLOSURE AND SHARING
RECOVERY STORIES

The term *self-disclosure* refers to anything you say as part of peer counseling in which you reveal information about your personal experience or life. Peer Support Specialists are required to be willing to disclose information about themselves and their recovery when it is appropriate. Recovery stories are a great example of self-disclosure, but there are many others, including:

- What you say about yourself when you introduce yourself to clients.

- Passing comments you make about your background, education, family, or personal interests.

- Sharing your personal thoughts or feelings about any topic, whether related or unrelated to your client's recovery.

- Comments you make about your own experience of your work with that client or other clients. This would include disclosing what you have learned from the client or your feelings about them.

Self-disclosure is a very powerful tool in peer counseling. It will be one of your most important ways to help your client recover. Because of that, it is essential that you are clear on why you are using it. Consider the following positive uses for self-disclosure:

1. **It Is a Way to Share Information.** When you share your experience, you are providing information to your client—it can be about an illness, a clinical service, or something about recovery.

2. **It Is a Way to Share an Experience.** People need to know about the personal experiences of others in similar situations. By sharing yours, you are likely changing their view of theirs.

3. **It Builds the Connection Between You and Your Client.** By sharing personal information, you make it easier for your client to know you and to feel a connection to you as a peer. That connection is key to being helpful to your client.

4. **It Maintains Your Status as a Peer.** Clients may start to see you as a clinician or as an "expert." This is a danger in peer counseling, since your relationship as a peer is what makes peer counseling effective. By sharing personal information, you can undercut the tendency of some clients to change that peer relationship into something different.

5. **It Is a Way to Model Behavior.** Peer Support Specialists have an invaluable role in modeling recovery

for their clients. By sharing personal information, you are helping your clients see how you do things, giving them a model for their own behavior. This does not mean that you should feel pressure to share only how you are successful. You want to model being open and non-defensive, and so sharing your successes and failures will have a bigger impact than presenting yourself as only successful.

6. **It Is a Way to Negotiate Your Relationship with Your Client.** It is not uncommon that you will hit snags in relationships with some clients. They may do things that confuse you or make you angry. You may do things that frustrate them or that they misunderstand. Talking openly with clients about those interactions and your response to them will be part of keeping your relationship growing and modeling good communication.

There are also dangers to self-disclosure. If the client is not ready or not comfortable with what you disclose, they may pull back from working with you. Self-disclosure involves temporarily focusing the conversation on you and your experience. If you do this too much, the client may feel that the peer counseling has become an opportunity for you to talk about yourself, rather than time for them. If you disclose too openly, you may make the client feel anxious and vulnerable.

To ensure you are using self-disclosure in a way that helps your client, consider the following suggestions:

- Track how much of the peer counseling conversation is spent on your self-disclosure, including your recovery stories. Most of the conversation should involve the client talking about themselves. If you are talking, on average, more than 50 percent of the time, you are likely using self-disclosure too much.

- Be focused. Self-disclosures that are long and rambling risk distracting from the peer counseling and reducing your client's interest. Every sentence in your disclosure should have a purpose related to the peer counseling. Be succinct and to the point.

- Consider and track your client's reactions to your self-disclosure. A good self-disclosure will result in the client talking more about themselves and being more engaged in the conversation. An unhelpful self-disclosure will result in the client talking less and looking confused, anxious, or frustrated.

- Be attentive to your own feelings about why you are self-disclosing. Are you sharing to help the peer counseling or because it feels good to talk about yourself and your accomplishments or struggles? Use your feelings to guide your efforts to stay focused on the client and their recovery.

EFFECTIVE RECOVERY STORIES

Effective Peer Support Specialists often use stories about their own experience with a problem, with using treatment, or with recovery in order to engage, guide, and support their clients. An effective recovery story can make a number of possible contributions to peer counseling:

1. **It Educates Your Client.** A good recovery story includes information that your client can use in their efforts to recover. It may include factual details, like what symptoms you experienced or what services you found helpful. You may also offer information about the experience of illness, treatment, or recovery. Clinicians typically don't talk about the experiential aspects of illness, and so this may be the most valuable part you will

contribute.

2. **It Builds the Client's Hope.** A good recovery story points to the reality that there is always potential to recover, and that it is possible for anyone to take the difficult steps needed to do so. Most clients will be struggling with hope. As a Peer Support Specialist, you are concrete evidence that recovery can happen. Make sure your story includes the following:

   - A description of the experience of having the illness.

   - The steps that you or others took to address the illness and its effects on your life, so that your client can see how the recovery was achieved.

   - The experience of recovery, particularly the benefits, so that your client can see that this is possible and worthwhile to achieve.

3. **It Connects the Client to You and Other Supports.** A good recovery story helps the client continue to build a personal connection to you as a peer counselor, increasing that all-important sense of trust and rapport. Trust builds over time and will give you more potential to influence them in future conversations.

THE KEY ELEMENTS OF A GOOD RECOVERY STORY

Effective recovery stories have several things in common.

- Any good story has a beginning, a middle, and an end. The beginning of the story introduces the setting, the characters, and the situation. The situation is usually the health or life problems you had to deal with. The middle of the story builds the tension: How did you try to overcome the problem over time? What worked and what did not? What key successes and setbacks did you experience? The end of the story resolves the struggle, explains how you addressed the situation, and clarifies what you learned and what benefits you earned by recovering. Important loose ends in the story are typically tied up by the conclusion.

- The story you choose to tell should focus on the needs of the client, and not so much about what you want to say. New Peer Support Specialists often make the mistake of telling recovery stories that focus more on what they want to say than on what the client needs to hear. It may feel good to tell others about yourself, but does it help the client?

- The story is clear and focused. Most good recovery stories are simple and easily understandable, maintaining a central theme throughout. A common mistake is including too much detail or allowing the story to meander in a way that leaves the listener confused about what you are trying to say.

- The story is real—you are telling your client about your actual personal experience. Sharing your recovery story is an opportunity for personal connection. Clients can tell when you are being real and most will respond better to an honest telling of your story. Be wary of any temptation to embellish or distort your story, as this can undermine your credibility. By sharing personal, even vulnerable details, you can help the client know that you are being genuine.

- The story is respectful of your client. Recovery stories are often very personal. A common mistake is including content that is so personal that it makes your client uncomfortable. It is not always a bad thing to feel a little uncomfortable, but you will only want to do it in a way that makes the story more effective. Ask for feedback from other Peer Support

Specialists to help you ensure that your stories are respectful. You may want to write out your most common recovery stories and ask for feedback on them from others.

COMMON TYPES OF RECOVERY STORIES

You will have many opportunities to tell recovery stories, and so you want variations of your stories that focus on different themes. These variations will address the different needs of various clients. You pick the theme that will most likely be useful for different groups and individuals. Common themes include:

1. **The Experience of the Illness or Problem.** Clients often feel that they are alone or isolated in their experience of their problem or illness. Your story can help break that sense of isolation. It can also help them recognize other symptoms that they have not seen as part of their problem.

2. **Engaging in Treatment and Working with Providers.** This is often a critical need of our clients. Research suggests that most people tend to be slow to get the treatment and support that we need in a timely way. An account of how you engaged successfully in care will be useful in encouraging them to move more quickly to get the help they need. Stories that include challenges in dealing with providers or the healthcare system will help your clients understand that this is common and that their persistence will likely be required.

3. **The Recovery Process.** You can describe the recovery process from the beginning of the clinical need, to recognition of the need, initial efforts to get help, experiences in treatment, successes and failures, eventual success, the experience of being in recovery, and lessons learned. This gives your client a picture of what may be ahead of them, making it easier for them to see a way

forward.

4. **The Importance of Persistence and Patience in Recovery/Treatment.** Successful recovery almost always includes setbacks. Some clients don't expect that and so feel like a failure when they experience a setback, which can cause them to give up or to make poor decisions about recovery and supports. We all need reminders that setbacks are part of recovery and that patience and perseverance are critical to successful recoveries.

5. **The Recovery Stories of Others.** As a Peer Support Specialist, you will hopefully talk with many other Peer Support Specialists and hear a wide range of recovery stories from them. Remember those stories and retell them when they will help your clients. Clients need to know that other people recover, too, and that you weren't just the only lucky one.

As a Peer Support Specialist, keep in mind that you'll encounter different clients in different settings, so think about the length, detail, and tone of your story, and change it to suit the various needs you are trying to address:

- **Short vs. Long Stories.** You will likely find it useful to have a one- to two-minute version of your story, a five-minute version, and a ten-minute version. Longer stories give opportunity for more detail but should merit the time they take. In very unusual situations, you may want a version that is longer than ten minutes.

- **Stories That Explain Something vs. Stories That Push for Something.** A good story meets the needs of the client. In some conversations, clients will primarily need to better understand what is happening to them. They won't understand the problem, or their reaction to the problem, or the reaction of other people. You can help them understand these things by using a good story. At other times, clients primarily need to be encouraged to take a step or to do something they are not doing. They may need to engage in some form of help. They may need to change something in their life. A good story about taking that step can help them to see its value and figure out how to take it.

- **Funny vs. Serious vs. Emotional Stories.** Recovery stories can have different "tones" depending on what the situation calls for. A funny version will often be very appealing, because people enjoy humor and yet learn important information. A serious version is ideal for situations in which the content is particularly important and merits extra emphasis. A version of your story that focuses on the emotional experience of recovery and that is shaped to draw out an emotional reaction from the audience is another way to alter the tone and to engage people in your story.

KEY DO'S AND DON'TS

- Do create a story that matches the need and the situation of your client. Don't tell a story if the focus, content, emotional tone, or length is not a match for where your client is.

- Do track and respond to the client while you are telling the story. Your client will give you clues to how they are feeling and what they are interested in. In particular, you will be able to see in their eyes if the story is making a good impact, or if they are bored, uncomfortable, or confused.

- Don't tell any story that is so long or so detailed that it loses focus, gets boring, or confuses your listener.

- Do transition from your story back to what the client is working on. It can be helpful to state what you hope the client learns from your story and then turn the conversation to their need.

Do get feedback on your recovery stories from your colleagues. Use that feedback to get better and better at telling effective recovery stories.

CHAPTER 12

IDENTIFYING A RECOVERY GOAL AND STAYING FOCUSED

There is a saying, often attributed to Charles Kettering of General Motors, that "a problem well stated is a problem half solved." The corollary is that "a goal well stated is a goal half achieved."

Peer counseling is a powerful tool to help people change. Clients and even peer counselors have difficulty at times staying focused on what specific change is most important. The danger is that the peer counseling conversations can shift and change between meetings, and even within meetings, in a way that undermines the process and limits the benefits.

Keeping focused on what the client is trying to accomplish will be of great value to both of you. That is not to say that the goal of peer counseling should never change, but when it does, it should be very clear to the client and the peer counselor that there is a change in focus and what the new goal is.

To be effective, the goal should be the client's. It reflects the heart of what the client wants to achieve. Goals that are framed in a desired achievable direction often are more motivating, and so I encourage clients to set goals focused in a positive way.

For example, consider the following revised goals:

- "I want to break up with my boyfriend, who is not good for me" can be restated to "I want to find a new romantic relationship that is healthier for me."
- "I want to stop fighting with my nurse practitioner" can be restated as "I want to better collaborate with my nurse practitioner in a way that improves the care I receive."
- "I want my peer support group to stop driving me crazy" can be restated as "I want to find a way to have a healthy positive experience in a peer support group, either my current group or a new group."

To make a goal more valuable, you may encourage clients to add one or more secondary goals that are more specific and that meet the criteria for a SMART goal. That is, it is

- **S**pecific
- **M**easurable
- **A**chievable
- **R**elevant
- **T**ime-bound

Examples of Goals. For a client's overall goal of "I want to go back to school and be successful," the following secondary goals can provide helpful detail:

1. "I want to enroll in Acme Community College by the start of this fall semester."

2. "I want to meet with the student disabilities office and gain their support in establishing accommodations that I need by the beginning of the fall semester."

3. "I want to meet with each of my professors individually and talk about what I need to be successful. I want to do this by the end of the second week of classes."

You can see in this example that the goals now set out specific tasks for the client. Those goals can then give direction to the peer counseling conversations. They also make it easier to see whether the client is making progress, and if not, to identify specific areas that they are having trouble with.

Ways to Use Goals. Goals are a tool that can be used to encourage recovery. Consider the following ways to use goals:

1. Ask about the overall goal in the first meeting. Document it in your first note in the client's own words.

2. Revisit and refine that goal in the early meetings, and add specific SMART secondary goals. Document these so that you can refer to them.

3. Check back in with the client periodically about the goals, asking them to review how they feel about them and their progress toward meeting them. This may lead to a revision of the goals. Document that change.

4. If the client talks at length about issues that are not related to the goal, consider whether you should remind the client of the goals set for the peer counseling, and ask how this new topic relates to their goals. Some clients have a chaotic style of thinking about issues, and you will see this in how they deal with their own goals. I try to

point that out to clients (e.g., "You said your goal was to enroll in college, but now we've spent the entire meeting talking about your conflict with your sister. Last week you talked mostly about your new pet. You seem to be having trouble staying focused on what you want to change . . . is that something you've noticed before?").

5. Add new goals or subgoals as it becomes clear that the client wants to expand their work. Document those and refer back to them.

6. As your client starts to move toward ending the peer counseling, remind them of their goals and review their progress in meeting them. Help them see what they have achieved and to appreciate their own progress.

7. In cases where you think it is time to end the peer counseling, you can review the goals with the client as a way to talk about ending. If they've achieved their goals, you can say, "It looks like we've successfully completed your goals, and so now would be the natural place to stop." If they've not reached their goals, you could say, "It looks like we haven't been successful with your original goals. You may want to continue to work on those, or maybe those aren't as important as they seemed when we started. Anyway, it seems like this might be a place to stop. What do you think?"

8. When you document your last peer counseling discussion, include a reference to the client's original goals and comment on their degrees of success at meeting those goals.

CHAPTER 13

USING RECOVERY GOALS TO GUIDE PROBLEM-SOLVING

We've talked about the importance of having a clear overall goal for guiding the peer counseling work. This summary goal will ensure that you and your client are working on the same issue and that you'll know whether you are making progress.

In many cases you'll also want to use problem-solving strategies in the peer counseling conversations, as they can help add focus and effectiveness. Consider these steps to effective problem-solving.

DEFINING A PROBLEM

This can be more difficult than it may seem. You want to help the client create a clear definition of what it is they want to change. Problems often have multiple layers, and so when the first definition is stated, the client may recognize that there is another layer below that. When that is carefully stated, another layer may become clear.

For example, a client may initially say, "I want to go back to work. I haven't worked since my last hospitalization and I need to go back." As you talk with them, they realize that the problem underlying the need to return to work is that they hate the type of work they've been doing and don't want to do that anymore. They say the real problem is "I need to find a new type of work to do that I am good at and that I like." As they talk about this, they realize that they know what types of work they want to do but will need additional schooling to qualify for those jobs. They now feel that the goal is to go back to school.

Defining a problem accurately is a key part of solving it, so it is worth spending the time to clarify what the real problem is and then turning it into a measurable goal.

GENERATING POSSIBLE SOLUTIONS

Brainstorming solutions is the next common step. The term *brainstorming* refers to the strategy of generating a list of possible solutions to a problem. A key element in brainstorming is the purposeful suspension of any effort to evaluate the solutions being generated. This creates a no-risk situation in which people can be particularly creative and look for possible solutions outside the box. Suspending evaluation of the suggestions can be very difficult for people, but it is important, as the ability to generate innovative solutions will be greatly reduced as soon as someone starts to make evaluative comments like "That will never work." I find that I usually have to remind people who are brainstorming that they are not supposed to be evaluating any comments until later.

SELECTING A SOLUTION TO TRY

After brainstorming is completed, you and your client have hopefully generated a significant number of possible solutions. The next phase is to evaluate those possible solutions so that you can identify the most promising to try. You will typically be evaluating the solutions based on two criteria: (1) how likely they are to solve the problem and (2) how practical they are to implement.

Consider this example: The client wants to start dating but doesn't know any eligible people to ask out. Together, you and your client brainstorm possible solutions, including the following:

1. The client could ask their friends if they know of anyone who would be open to a casual date.
2. The client could sign up on a dating website.
3. The client could hire a matchmaking service.
4. The client could ask their religious leader for help in finding someone to ask.

Together you rate these solutions for how likely they are to result in a date and how practical they are to implement. Option 2 appears both probable and practical. Options 1 and 4 are practical, but your client doesn't think their friends or their rabbi can really help, so they are not likely solutions. Option 3 is probable but not practical—matchmaker services are too expensive for your client. So, the option with the top total rating is option 2 because it is both practical and will probably result in success.

TRYING THE FIRST SOLUTION

Now you and your client try the top-rated solution. You want to ensure that solution is given a real effort. If it is not implemented well, then your client is likely to not have a successful outcome. More problematic, they won't be able to tell if they did not succeed because it was the wrong solution or because they didn't actually do a good job trying it.

Consider this example: Your client wants to return to school but must find a way to pay for tuition. Together you generate ten different ways to pay for school, with the most promising solution being that they would apply for tuition reimbursement from the state rehabilitation services program. To try this strategy, they go online to research the guidelines for how to apply. When you meet with them, your client says, "I tried to figure out their website—it is terrible! I couldn't figure out how to apply or even if I qualify. I think that is not going to work out. Let's try a different strategy."

They have not really tried this strategy. Is your client's frustration evidence that this strategy won't work or that your client does not have much hope and is ready to give up easily? Without further effort by the client, they'll not be able to evaluate whether this strategy will work.

EVALUATING THE OUTCOME AND REVISING THE PLAN

Assuming that your client successfully implements the first strategy to solve their problem, it is important now to clearly review the outcome of that effort. Did the solution produce the outcome that your client wanted? Did it create any other problems that your client didn't expect? Do they think this is the solution they now want to use?

Often, the first solution does not fully work or produces additional unanticipated problems, and so your client will want to try a new solution. You'll want to help them go back to the list of solutions and choose another possible strategy to try. Again, be sure to give the next solution the same amount of effort so that you will be able to see if it can be successful.

It is not uncommon for the second try to also be unsuccessful. Your client's next step is to go to the third strategy and give that a try. Each trial is likely to generate new information that your client can use to design better possible solutions. Some clients (and peer counselors) can become discouraged with solutions that don't work. As the peer counselor, your job is to remain positive and encouraging so that your client will persevere long enough to see whether any solution will actually work.

USING PROBLEM-SOLVING LANGUAGE TO GUIDE YOUR CLIENT

This problem-solving strategy may solve your client's problem. But even if it does not, it will provide your client with some clear concepts that will help the peer counseling be more effective. For example, by clearly defining the problem, your client will make progress toward solving it. By setting SMART goals, your client will be clearer on what they need to do, and whether they are doing it. By talking about possible solutions, your client will see that most problems are complex, and solutions can take a lot of shapes. This often helps them see that they can be more creative than they have been, and that more strategies are open to them than they thought. By trying solutions and measuring outcomes, your client will better understand what actual success looks like and what they need to do for any solution to work. The overall approach will help your client be a clearer thinker, which will help the peer counseling be more focused. This approach also builds hope; the focus on what the client wants and the practical, persistent effort to achieve it will help the client see that they can make progress.

CHAPTER 14

SHARING INFORMATION

Often your clients won't have the information they need to make a good decision about their recovery. As a Peer Support Specialist, you'll have a growing library of information that is helpful to others. Unfortunately, if you are not thoughtful about how you share it, you are likely to sound like a know-it-all, which becomes a barrier to your clients.

ASKING FOR PERMISSION

In general, no one appreciates unsolicited advice or information. We often interpret this advice as other people butting into our affairs and as disrespectful. The result is that we resist what the other person says.

There is a simple and effective strategy to avoid that defensiveness. Simply ask for permission to share information. "Would it be OK if I shared some information with you that I have found to be helpful?" or "I have some information that I think is relevant to what we are talking about. Would it be OK if I shared that with you?"

People virtually never say no. By asking the question, you are showing your client respect and reminding them that you see them as a separate person who is responsible for solving their own problems and making their own decisions. Most importantly, you are avoiding the common result of them feeling defensive and not accepting the information.

FRAMING THE INFORMATION

Your client will want to know where you got this information. If it is factual, you will want to use well-recognized authorities such as the National Institutes of Health, Centers for Disease Control, and the National Alliance on Mental Illness. If the information is about people's experience, you will want to be clear as to whether you are talking about your experience or about what other people have told you about their experience.

Another part of framing information is to say what you think the information should mean to your client. This is an interpretation on your part, but your client will often appreciate it, as they will be able to better make sense of the information. For example, if you are sharing the fact that long-term alcohol use is associated with a shortened life span, you might frame that fact as "This information highlights one of the risks of using alcohol that many people don't know about."

LOOKING FOR THEIR RESPONSE

You will want to watch for your client's reaction to the information you've shared. You'll be able to see whether they understand the information and whether it has moved them forward in any way. You'll also want to watch for any evidence that the information has left them feeling defensive or frustrated.

You may want to consider doing some repair if they have responded poorly.

COLLECTING INFORMATION TO SHARE

Given your job, you'll want to get in the habit of collecting information that your clients will find helpful in their effort to recover. This will be a continuous endeavor, as what is known about illnesses, treatments, and recovery changes fairly rapidly these days. Consider adopting the following strategies to build and maintain a current knowledge base that you can use in your sessions:

1. Get in a habit of attending continuing education offerings. There are in-person and virtual learning opportunities available to you. The key is to pursue those most relevant for your work and work setting.

2. Participate in other trainings available at your work site. Most clinical programs recognize the importance of ongoing education for their staff. Be sure you are part of these. While they will be targeted at you as a Peer Support Specialist, always consider what information may be helpful for your clients.

3. Consider getting comfortable looking at research summaries. You can easily find the current research on any topic by using search engines such as Google Scholar or PubMed. Most research articles have a summary, called an *abstract*, at the start of the article, telling you everything important about the study. I know Peer Support Specialists who feel intimidated by research studies and research language, but you'll want to fight that feeling. Researchers do use a lot of jargon, though they are almost always talking about fairly simple concepts that you can definitely understand and use. Don't get intimidated.

Recognize the importance of "experiential" information, which is not going to be found in any research article. Rather, it's the experience people have with recovery or with different illnesses or treatments. Look to your own experience, the experience of other Peer Support Specialists, and other people you know who are in recovery.

You may also want to build your experience with virtual libraries of treatment and recovery stories. For example, the Make the Connection website (www.maketheconnection.net) has a large collection of recovery stories from individual people, organized by illness, stage of recovery, and background of the person (age, race, gender, etc.). YouTube also has a large number of recovery stories, but these are of a more mixed quality.

CHAPTER 15

RECOGNIZING WHEN MORE HELP IS NEEDED

A key skill for any type of peer counseling is to recognize when your client needs more help and/or more advanced help than you can give. This is a rather common situation—not a failure on your part—that every clinician and Peer Support Specialist needs to handle successfully if their clients are to get what they need.

We talked earlier about the boundaries of what peer counseling is and when it is helpful. When the client or the situation calls for an intervention beyond peer counseling, a good peer counselor quickly recognizes it and helps the client add that type of support.

COMMON MARKERS

You should always be watching for the following signs that additional help is needed:

1. **The Client Is Getting Significantly Worse Despite Your Best Efforts.** Symptoms often increase and

decrease over time. When they get worse in a way that significantly raises the risk to your client, you will want to consider seeking additional help. Your supervisor will be the best source of guidance on whether added help is needed. The client may feel a need for more help, but they may also not want help even though they need it.

2. **You Feel That You Don't Understand What Is Happening in the Sessions.** It is very common to feel confused at points in peer counseling conversations. When you notice that you don't understand what is happening over most of the session or over multiple sessions, it may be a sign that the client needs additional services. Again, your supervisor will be a great help in understanding what is happening and how best to respond.

3. **In Response to a New Stressor, the Client Appears to Be Going into a Significant Crisis.** New stressors can push clients into a more serious crisis. You want to always consider whether your client has the resources they need to address the challenges they are facing. If new stressors call for more help, you will want to move quickly to pull in those resources.

4. **The Content in Your Peer Counseling Sessions Tends to Focus on Symptoms or Topics That You Don't Know Much About.** We all have strengths and weaknesses. If you find that your client is talking more about things that you are not good at helping with, or that you don't know much about, it is responsible to ask yourself whether your client would be better served in working with a different Peer Support Specialist, who has the skills that match their needs. Again, this is not evidence of a failure but rather a sign that you know what

you are and are not good at. In the peer support teams I've had the privilege of working with, different members had different areas of expertise. Clients could be referred to the Peer Support Specialists with experience in those different areas to ensure they had the most qualified support. If your team is small, be careful to work with your supervisor about how to deal with situations outside your experience and/or training.

5. **You Feel Like You Can't Give the Person What They Need.** There are situations in which, despite your best efforts, it will appear that you are not able to give the client what they need. You may be providing supports that have worked well with other clients, but not with this client. That feeling that you just can't seem to give the client what they need is one of those valuable pieces of information that can help you recognize that there is just something missing. Sometimes clients need a change. Sometimes *you* will need a change. Regardless of the reason, it is always worth considering if you should pull in another Peer Support Specialist or some other type of clinical help. Your supervisor will be a great resource in thinking these situations through.

CHALLENGES TO RECOGNIZING THE NEED FOR MORE HELP

The biggest challenge to recognizing when we should pull in additional help is our own fear of looking or feeling like we are not good at our work. I find this is a very common feeling among new Peer Support Specialists. They often think that if they are competent, then they should be able to successfully meet the needs of every client they have. This is a very unrealistic expectation that we all fall victim to at times. Experienced Peer Support Specialists have learned that they can't meet the needs of everyone, and they don't need to. Our clients are best served when we recognize—and use—all the resources on our teams. Seasoned peers ask for help often, and their clients benefit from that approach.

HOW TO DRAW IN ADDITIONAL SUPPORTS

Each clinical setting will have procedures for how to pull in additional supports for your client. You'll want to use those procedures. You will also want to talk about these situations with your supervisor, who will have insights into how to do this, and what supports you may want to consider. If you are working on a clinical team, these situations are good topics for discussion by the entire team. One of the benefits of working in teams is the varied input from different perspectives by team members. These situations are often complex, and so your team's input may help you find the best supports for the client.

CHAPTER 16

BEING AWARE OF YOURSELF

In any peer counseling conversation, you will be receiving information about your client not only through what they say but how they act, their body language, the way they talk, and even what they don't say. A lot of information is coming in, and sometimes the most important is not what is being said. Recognizing and using that information is an advanced peer counseling skill.

You are likely to find that your feelings during a conversation can be a valuable source of information about the client. Sometimes this reflects what you are indirectly picking up about the client— some might call that intuition. It can also be more about you than the client. You may be reacting to what the client said because of your own history or unresolved issues. You don't want to confuse your own issues with the client's, so you want to be clear on why you are reacting the way you are. Talking with your supervisor can help in working with your reactions and clarifying which are really just about you.

Your reactions may tell you about the client, their problem, and how they are relating to you. Sometimes your reaction will give you important clues that you are not quite aware of or that don't match what the client is saying. You can use that information to better understand your client, to identify things that are not being said but that are important, and keep track of how well you are connecting with the client. Some common examples include:

1. **When You Feel Bored with a Client.** This does not mean that the client is a boring person. What it usually means is that the conversation is boring; it is missing something that most peer counseling conversations have. You may find that you feel bored when the client is not really talking about anything important or not being honest in the conversation. That feeling can help you recognize that something is unsaid or missing in the client's motivation. It might be something you've done or something they are doing to derail the real conversation that is needed. It is usually a sign that you need to back up and figure out what is missing.

2. **When You Feel Confused by a Client.** Clients will talk about many different topics and some complex experiences. You may feel confused if they have not explained things well. You may also feel confused if the client is confused. If they are confused by their own mixed feelings, then you as the peer counselor may begin to feel what they are feeling. You may want to respond by saying something like, "I feel very confused by what we are talking about, and I'm not sure why. Are these topics confusing for you?"

3. **When You Feel Surprisingly Worried About a Client.** You may work with clients who appear to be doing well, but you notice that you have a growing feeling of worry

about them. The feeling doesn't match the content of what they are saying. I encourage you to take those feelings seriously and look for reasons that you are worried. The client may not be aware of, or sharing their concerns, but you may still be seeing them in an indirect way. Look for ways that they are at risk that they are not talking about. In some situations, you might share that experience with the client, though not always. You might say something like, "I find myself feeling worried about the peer counseling. You seem to be doing well, and so I'm wondering if my worry is a sign that there is something that we've not talked about that is a real concern."

4. **When You Feel Afraid of a Client.** You may occasionally come across a client who is dangerous in some way, whether physically or psychologically. While they may not say or do anything threatening, in some situations, you may just start to feel afraid of the person. Again, you are likely picking up on indirect cues that this person is a danger. You want to take those feelings seriously and act on them. Talk with your supervisor and your peers to make sure you understand why you are feeling that way. If appropriate, take extra precautions to enhance your safety. Your supervisor will be key in helping you do that effectively.

LISTENING TO YOUR REACTIONS

As a peer counselor, you want to get in the habit of tracking your feelings and reactions during any peer counseling conversation. It should be a running monitor in your head. Most of the time, these reactions will be entirely consistent with what is being said. It is when they don't match that you want to pay particular attention. Here are a few strategies that may be helpful:

1. Track how your body feels. Are you surprisingly tense, worried, excited?

2. Track your thoughts about the session. Are you looking forward to getting out of the conversation? Are you feeling helpless about making any progress?

3. Talk with your supervisor and trusted peers about your reactions. Listen to their input about what these reactions might mean.

ANALYZING YOUR REACTIONS

Your reactions can reflect one of two very different things. As we talked about earlier, they can reflect your reaction to information you are picking up in the conversation about your client. Those are the most valuable situations, as they add to what you know about your client and so can help you be more effective.

Your reactions can also reflect you and your own issues that are being triggered by what the client is saying. We all have our own personal issues, and conversations in peer counseling sessions can trigger them. For example, you may have a past experience of trauma, and your client may be talking about their own trauma in a way that triggers your feelings about your experience. Your reaction is partly about the client, but really it is more about you. It is always worth asking, "Is my reaction about my client or about me? Is my reaction telling me something useful about them or me?"

If the answer is that your reaction is really about you, you will want to talk with your supervisor about this. It is very predictable that this will happen, but you want to become more able to recognize those reactions and not confuse them with reactions about the client. Even more important, you want to use them to further your own recovery.

CHAPTER 17

HELPING YOUR CLIENT REWRITE THEIR STORY

People are naturally oriented toward stories and narrative. We automatically create stories out of our experience. Sometimes those stories are helpful, but some can also result in problems. For example, your clients will come to you with at least one, and sometimes multiple, stories explaining the difficulties they are facing. Those stories may reflect what others have said to them (e.g., "You drink so much because you are a selfish person!"). They may have a story that reflects what healthcare providers have said to them (e.g., "Your drinking is a 'disease' that is caused by genetics—that's why your parents also drank"). They may have come up with their own story (e.g., "I have a drinking problem because my girlfriend dumped me").

Peer counseling often involves conversations that cause clients to rewrite their stories related to their problem/illness, treatment, and recovery. This happens automatically whether you are aware of it or not. It is better to recognize it and embrace your role in helping your client revise and rewrite their stories. Consider the following assumptions about stories:

1. Our personal stories reflect the stories told by the groups we belong to, including family, friends, the media, communities, countries, religions, and cultures. The clinical community and the self-help community use stories heavily in how they explain mental health problems, solutions to those problems, and the process of recovery.

2. Stories are not "objective truth" but constructed ideas that can have value in explaining things or suggesting what we should do. Most people have multiple stories that explain the same experience. They hold and use these simultaneously. The different stories can be useful in different ways. The concept that only one story can be "true" is a story in itself and is often not helpful.

3. Problems occur when the stories people have about themselves do not fit with their lived experience. The mismatch between the stories and the experience can cause confusion and stress. It is often a sign that the stories need to change to include new or different experiences.

4. The concepts of mental illnesses, often portrayed as "real" scientific entities, can be seen as part of a story.

5. Some people can get into difficult places when their lives have become tied too closely to a single story that is either limiting and/or superficial rather than multiple stories or more complex and nuanced stories.

6. Recovery always involves people changing the story or stories that they are using to understand themselves and their lives.

7. Effective clinical treatment and peer support involve ways of helping people change their stories so that recovery is supported. Participation in treatment and peer support can have direct benefits, but also creates benefits by being part of a story of change.

8. Peer Support Specialists have a particularly powerful role in helping clients change their stories. Because of their shared experience of illness and recovery, clients will see Peer Support Specialists as having more insight, more credibility, and so more authority when it comes to rewriting a "true" story.

A common pattern in recovery is that people broaden their stories to include a wider range of factors that contribute to their problem and to their recovery. A client who initially thinks that their depression is caused by them being "a lazy person" may change that story to understand that their depression is related to a number of things, including their genetics, their physical health and lifestyle (diet and exercise), the way their spouse treats them, the way they treat themselves, problems with their work environment, and even the way they are treated in their community.

That broadening of the story has a number of benefits:
- It provides more factors that can be addressed to improve the problem.

- It often reduces inappropriate shame and self-blame.

- It often helps clarify which factors are outside and which are inside the client's control, helping them see their choices and responsibilities more clearly.

- It often results in increased insight, curiosity, and hope.

Peer counseling involves listening to people tell their story, you as the peer counselor sharing your story, followed by ongoing discussions that result in both you and your client revising your stories. In terms of how to ensure the conversation is helpful for your client, consider the following strategies:

1. Start with the client and their story, told from their perspective. Counseling emphasizes listening because you want to start with their current version of their story. You want to hear it and you want them to hear it. Listen for how they define "the problem." Listen for how they explain the cause of the problem—what role did they play?

2. Share your story about your recovery from your perspective. Be thoughtful about your own story, including how you define "the problem," what events and people you include in the story, what role you played, and what your explanation is for what caused the problem and what led to your recovery.

3. The conversation should be mutual—you want your client to be open and curious about their story, and so you want to be open and curious as well. A real conversation will likely involve back-and-forth discussion, new ideas about important factors in the story, and an eventual change in the way each of you consider the story.

4. Consider including broader factors in the discussion. How has family contributed to their story? How has their community contributed? How about economics or culture?

5. Help them identify any stories they've gotten from the healthcare community. Help them see any strengths and limitations in those.

6. Encourage them to include their strengths and resources in their story. Clients will often overlook the resources they bring and the strengths they've shown in their stories. Point those out.

7. Help your client see important things they are leaving out of their story. This could include other elements of the problem, choices they made, things they didn't do.

8. Help your client identify the factors that were/are outside their control and those that were/are within their control. Clients will often confuse these, leaving them feeling responsible for things they can't change and unaware of the things they can change.

Intentional Peer Support (www.intentionalpeersupport.org) is both an organization and a perspective on peer support that focuses heavily on how peer support can lead to people rewriting their stories. They describe their goal as helping peer support providers "learn to use relationships to see things from new angles, develop greater awareness of personal and relational patterns, and support and challenge each other in trying new things." They emphasize that peer support involves mutual revision of our understanding of our experience, through ongoing open discussions between Peer Support Specialists and their clients. They express particular concern about the limitations that come from the stories that clinical providers and the clinical community encourage. I would recommend that you explore their resources to better build your skills in this area.

CHAPTER 18

ADVANCED REFLECTIONS AND SUMMARIES

As the client makes efforts to try to achieve their peer counseling goals, you are likely to understand more about why they are struggling than they will. You may see behaviors that create barriers for them. You may recognize thoughts and feelings they may have, that undermine their efforts. This is a natural result of working with anyone and creates important opportunities for you to help them gain insight. Remember, it does not matter if you recognize these barriers. It only matters if your client understands them and uses that understanding to change.

We want to go back to our listening skills and add some advanced techniques. The difference between the basic reflections and summaries we talked about in chapters 8 and 9 and the advanced reflections and summaries described in this chapter is the amount of new information you add in your statements. In a basic reflection or summary, you are mostly, or entirely, telling the client what they have actually said. In an advanced reflection or summary, you are adding information that they've not said. For example, consider the following situation.

Client: "I am probably going to quit going to that smoking cessation support group. The other people don't listen to me and I don't feel like I fit in. It's frustrating, because support groups don't work for me—I always end up quitting. They work for other people but not me."

Example of a Basic Reflection: "You are thinking of quitting your support group. You don't feel like you fit, and this has happened before."

Examples of Advanced Reflections
1. "You are thinking about quitting another support group. You are again having trouble fitting in. They don't seem to be good listeners, but you are also wondering why this keeps happening to you and if it could be something you are doing."

2. "You are thinking about quitting another support group. You feel like there is a pattern here for you, but you don't understand it. You are wondering if there is something you could do differently that would make these groups work for you."

3. "You are thinking about quitting another support group. You are wondering if there is something you could do differently that would make these groups work for you. While we've been working together, you've tried to join two new groups. In both cases, you ended up arguing with people you met. Maybe trying to avoid early conflict might make it easier to join these groups."

You can see that the advanced reflections and summaries add something that the person may be feeling or thinking but did not really say. The first advanced reflection adds that "you are also wondering why this keeps happening to you and if it could be something you are doing." The second goes a little further, suggesting they are wondering if there is something they could do differently to make these groups work for them. The client did not say these things, but if you think they are thinking them, it can be helpful to say them out loud. The third reflection includes your observation about what they have done that contributes to the problem. This pushes them further, but hopefully they know this observation is correct and they trust that you are saying this to help them solve their problem.

You should be able to see quickly if you are right that they are thinking this. If they are, they will respond to this advanced reflection in the same way that they do when they are feeling heard. If you are wrong and they are not thinking this, you will see confusion or frustration in their eyes, and you can correct your reflection.

Advanced reflections and summaries help move the conversation forward, as you are including information that they are not saying but are feeling or thinking. They should be used only when you have already established trust by being a good listener and using basic reflections and summaries to prove you really understand them. Starting peer counseling relationships with advanced reflections and summaries almost never works, as the client has not learned to trust you and you've not proven that you understand them enough to offer interpretations.

FEELINGS

Like you do in basic reflections and summaries, your advanced reflections and summaries will focus at times on feelings, but these are unspoken feelings. For example, the client may say they are irritated about something, but you may think it is clear that they are more than irritated—they are quite angry. Your advanced reflection could include the idea that they are actually quite angry.

The client may also not even say anything about the feeling. Because you've been listening well to them, you have a pretty good idea that they are very hurt and angry, but that they don't want to say it. Your advanced reflection could include something like, "This situation is puzzling to you. You seem to feel hurt and angry about it." If you are right about that feeling, they will agree with the reflection and start to talk about those feelings. If you have it wrong, they are likely to disagree or look puzzled. You then have a chance to try to find the right feeling to reflect. Again, advanced reflections and summaries that include unspoken feelings can be very helpful to the client and can move the conversation forward.

THOUGHTS

Sometimes it is thoughts that are unspoken. In the example of the client who is dropping out of a support group, they may be thinking that there is something wrong with how they act in these groups. They didn't say that specifically, but it could be the unspoken interpretation behind what they did say to you. If you have listened to them well up to this point, you may have a clear sense that this is what they are thinking but not saying. By including these thoughts in your reflection or summary, you will move the conversation forward.

ACTIONS

Advanced reflections and summaries can also include comments about actions that the client is not saying but implying. Going back to our example, you might want to say something like, "You are wondering if you are doing something that leads to your difficulties in these support groups."

Advanced reflections and summaries always go beyond what the client has actually said, including thoughts, feelings, or actions that may be part of their experience. You are always making an educated guess about what you include. Because of this, you will be wrong some of the time. That is to be expected, so you want to be ready and able to backtrack when you are wrong or when the client is not ready to hear your comment. Backtracking will show that you understand that your comment did not feel accurate to your client and that you want to stay with their experience. If you keep pushing your interpretation or guess after they've responded negatively to it, you put your trust and rapport at risk.

EXERCISE 6: ADVANCED REFLECTIONS AND SUMMARIES

For each of the following scenarios from a hypothetical client, write down at least two possible advanced reflections. Be sure to include content that you think is likely true but is beyond what the client actually said. Examples of possible answers can be found in Appendix B.

<table>
<tr><td colspan="2">1. Your client is talking about a close friend who treats them poorly. They say this is a pattern over many years. Your client says they want to confront their friend but doesn't feel "ready."

You think that your client is not saying that they have very few friends and feel lonely often.</td></tr>
<tr><td>Possible Advanced Reflection #1</td><td></td></tr>
<tr><td>Possible Advanced Reflection #2</td><td></td></tr>
</table>

<table>
<tr><td colspan="2">2. Your client is talking about feeling a great deal of stomach pain over the past three weeks. They don't know what is causing it, but they have not called their doctor.

What you think is also true but your client is not saying: Their mother died of stomach cancer around the same age. Your client nursed her mother for the last months of her life and describes it as a "terrible experience."</td></tr>
<tr><td>Possible Advanced Reflection #1</td><td></td></tr>
<tr><td>Possible Advanced Reflection #2</td><td></td></tr>
</table>

<table>
<tr><td colspan="2">3. Your client is talking about returning to weekly meetings of Alcoholics Anonymous. They stopped going when they started dating their new girlfriend.

What you think is also true but your client is not saying: Your client has not told their girlfriend about their past problems with alcohol. They feel embarrassed about letting anyone know about this problem.</td></tr>
<tr><td>Possible Advanced Reflection #1</td><td></td></tr>
<tr><td>Possible Advanced Reflection #2</td><td></td></tr>
</table>

<table>
<tr><td colspan="2">4. Your client is talking about wanting to change psychiatrists. "Dr. White never listens to me. He's always pushing me to take medications. I don't think he likes me."

What you think is also true but your client is not saying: Your client was very stable on medications in the past and recently stopped taking any medications. Since that time, they have been complaining about symptoms and associated problems at work.</td></tr>
<tr><td>Possible Advanced Reflection #1</td><td></td></tr>
<tr><td>Possible Advanced Reflection #2</td><td></td></tr>
</table>

CHAPTER 19

CHALLENGING THOUGHTS AND ACTIONS

One of the more influential things you can do in a peer counseling session is to help the client reconsider what they think or have done. We all have thoughts and actions that don't fit with each other, and the inconsistencies are often important. If we don't see them, we are not likely to change them. Peer counselors can be valuable in helping clients identify and then change these inconsistencies.

WHEN TO DO IT

Challenging your client can stress or even destroy your helping relationship. For that reason, you'll usually do this after you've already built trust by listening well and being trustworthy. The more trust you have with your client, the more likely they will really listen to you when you challenge their thoughts or actions.

You'll want to look for situations in which your client is already wondering about their own thoughts and actions. They will be more open to your challenge in those situations. Challenging someone on a belief or action that they are strongly committed to is less likely to result in them actually hearing you or changing anything. Remind yourself to pick your battles, as there is a cost to failed challenges.

HOW TO DO IT

There is a wide range in how assertive you want to be in your challenges. Consider a peer counseling situation in which your client is saying that they really want to participate in treatment, but they also mention that they keep skipping meetings with their clinicians in order to do fun things. You might say one of the following:

1. "I hear that you are very committed to using treatment for your recovery, but I also hear that you are missing a lot of sessions. Help me understand that."

2. "So, you are very committed to treatment, but you've missed most of your sessions. Those don't fit together. What is going on with that?"

3. "It's hard to believe that you are actually committed to treatment and recovery when you keep skipping sessions to have fun. You need to think about what is keeping you out of treatment and how these fit with the overall goal we talked about."

The first comment is the gentlest and most tentative. It requires the least amount of trust. If the client is thoughtful and curious about themselves, it may be the easiest and best way to challenge their actions.

The second comment is a little more assertive and pointed in directing the client toward the inconsistency between their statements and their actions.

The third is the most assertive. It requires the highest level of trust so that the client does not simply respond by being defensive. It is the riskiest of the three. If the client rejects this challenge, it may hurt your rapport with them. But if they really hear you and can see your point, it can be helpful.

You can see in these examples that you are typically asking the person to notice inconsistencies in what they are saying and/or doing. By helping them notice these inconsistencies and encouraging them to be curious about their cause, you'll often help them see something that they are missing.

It is also possible that you simply don't understand something and that there is no inconsistency. Being heavy handed in a challenge that actually reflects that you don't understand the situation is often a very costly mistake.

WHAT TO AVOID

1. Don't make statements that imply you think poorly of them (e.g., "You are not committed to treatment. You just want to keep drinking!").

2. Don't make statements that imply that they should accept your challenge because you are "right" (e.g., "I have been around. I know that you are just avoiding treatment because you are afraid of recovery.").

3. Don't make the challenge about you versus them (e.g., "I don't think you are serious about recovery"). Instead, target the inconsistency in what they want and what they are doing.

4. Don't be rude or insulting. Dramatic confrontations can work occasionally, but you'll also destroy your trust with

many other clients (e.g., "You are full of shit! Come back when you are ready to be honest.").

LOOKING FOR THEIR RESPONSE

Challenges can be risky interventions. You'll want to watch your client for their reaction. The goal is for them to hear what you are saying and to at least become curious about what you are pointing out. You'll be able to see if that happens by what they say and how they act. Generally, you don't want them to respond by feeling offended and back off or become defensive. You'll also be able to see that by their reaction. If they do respond that way, you'll want to look for ways to repair any damage to trust and rapport.

EXERCISE 7: CHALLENGING THOUGHTS AND ACTIONS

For each of the following scenarios from a hypothetical client, write a challenge at the low, moderate, and high levels of assertiveness. You can look at sample responses in Appendix B for reference.

1. The client has complained to you repeatedly about how their husband is not honest about his feelings. They just described to you a situation in which *they* are not being honest about their feelings with their husband.	
Low Assertiveness	
Moderate Assertiveness	
High Assertiveness	

2. You hear from a clinical team member that your client has relapsed on alcohol. You have been talking with this client for months about their cravings and how to manage them. They come to see you but don't mention their relapse, presenting themselves as "doing well".

Low Assertiveness	
Moderate Assertiveness	
High Assertiveness	

3. Your client has been talking with you for weeks about their desire to have more friends to address their intense feelings of loneliness. It is their primary goal for peer counseling to make more friends. Today they tell you about some new people who are living in their building. When you ask if they have talked to them, your client says, "I am not really interested in talking to other people."

Low Assertiveness	
Moderate Assertiveness	
High Assertiveness	

<table>
<tr><td colspan="2">4. Your client regularly attends a peer support group. They complain to you every week about the group meetings, saying that they want the group to talk more about tension in the group. You ask your client if they have ever brought up the topic. They say, "I don't want to bring that topic up. Someone else should do it!"</td></tr>
<tr><td>Low Assertiveness</td><td></td></tr>
<tr><td>Moderate Assertiveness</td><td></td></tr>
<tr><td>High Assertiveness</td><td></td></tr>
</table>

CHAPTER 20

RECOGNIZING AND WORKING WITH AMBIVALENCE AND "RESISTANCE"

The term *ambivalence* is used in a variety of ways in the field of mental health, going back to Sigmund Freud. Ambivalence is common and natural. We are all ambivalent about many things, including things that are good for us. Most people are ambivalent about recovery and positive change. The practical implication for peer counselors is that if we expect or push for change when the client is very ambivalent but not ready for that change, they will push back. The pushback may manifest itself overtly, such as the client disagreeing with us, but it can be more indirect, such as skipping sessions or even discontinuing peer counseling.

It is essential to recognize that it's normal and common to push back when we feel ambivalent about change. It is almost always a sign that we feel threatened or uncomfortable with a potential change or treatment, and so we do something to protect ourselves. Some peers, particularly new Peer Support Specialists, interpret those actions as rejection or as "bad" behavior by their client. This is a common but costly misinterpretation, as it usually leads the peer to respond out of fear or anger.

RESISTANCE

Resistance is a loaded term that is often used to describe those actions clients take when they feel pushed by clinicians. It is not uncommon for clinicians to use the term to refer to a client's response they see as "not healthy" or as resisting healthy action that the clinician is pushing for. Unfortunately, I've seen it used to refer to any disagreement the client has with the clinician. We are all going to disagree with our clinicians at times. That is not *resistance*—but appropriate disagreement and assertiveness.

I think the most useful definition of *resistance* comes from Motivational Interviewing (MI), a common counseling approach to helping people change behaviors. From this view, resistance is defined as what happens when we expect or push for change when the client is not ready for it.

Resistance can take a number of forms. The most obvious is when you have a client who feels forced to be in treatment and who has no real interest in treatment or recovery. If they are direct with you, they may tell you outright that they have no interest in being in peer counseling or even talking with you, that they are there to avoid some consequence (jail, divorce, etc.) but don't believe they have any need to change. This form of resistance is obvious but relatively rare. The following are less direct but much more common:

1. **Denying Some Aspect of the Problem or Solution.** The client is not willing to fully acknowledge that they have a problem or that they need help. They may reframe their symptoms or problems as caused by someone else or by some other factor (e.g., "I'd be fine if my parents weren't so controlling"). They may make excuses for their behavior (e.g., "I'm drinking because I can't get to

sleep any other way!"). They may deny some aspect of the problem (e.g., "I'm not angry").

2. **Arguing with the Peer Counselor.** The peer counseling session may feel like a wrestling match, with your client disagreeing with you about basic facts or conclusions. They may question your methods or your authority to work as a Peer Support Specialist. They may use hostility to thwart the peer counseling.

3. **Interrupting and Diverting the Conversation.** The goal of this strategy is to indirectly disrupt the open discussion of the problems and solutions. The client may repeatedly interrupt you or may divert the conversation to topics that don't move the peer counseling forward.

4. **Passively Ignoring or Avoiding Participation.** The client may not show up for appointments or show up late. They may not pay attention or may ignore questions or comments. They may simply not take any initiative in directing the discussion. The client is using a passive stance toward protecting themselves.

"ROLLING WITH RESISTANCE"

The phrase "rolling with resistance" was coined by the founders of MI to describe a key strategy for responding to resistance. In these situations, it is very natural for the peer counselor to feel tempted to push the client harder. From an MI perspective, this is exactly the wrong step. When we directly push for change in a client who is ambivalent about it, they often push back. We may say why they should change, which simply reminds them of the reasons they should not.

When rolling with resistance, we should not respond to the client's resistance by increasing the arguments for making the change. Instead, we should use their statements of resistance to help them further explore the problem. Rolling with resistance keeps the conversation going, preventing the person from digging in to their stance. It reflects the core of a good helping stance, which is based in the reality that the client is the decider. They will make the decisions about any change to be made, and so our goal is to just be with them as they think about what they might do.

BEING PATIENT IN THE FACE OF RESISTANCE

Ambivalence and resistance are very common. You'll see them at some point in virtually every client. It is simply evidence that people are all ambivalent about change. For you as a peer counselor, the key to successfully working with resistance is to recognize and accept it, to understand what it means, and to patiently persist in the peer counseling while the client works out their feelings of ambivalence.

CHAPTER 21

RECOMMENDING, REFERRING, AND CONNECTING

Part of peer counseling involves helping people find and engage in the full range of supports and activities that can aid them in recovering a full life. Clinicians will often provide referrals to other types of formal treatment, but experienced Peer Support Specialists have the credibility and the network to help people engage with a larger array of supports, including clinical treatment, self-help groups, community-based social supports, and normal life activities that can be part of full community integration.

You are in a great position to introduce clients to other people, places, and activities that they need. Over time you will develop a large network of contacts inside and outside your organization that your clients may need. Be active and organized in developing that network, and take the time and effort to always be expanding and maintaining the contacts you've developed. You may find that you play this part in your clinical team, and that other members of your team ask you to connect clients to key resources. To do this well, you'll want to consider a few key strategies.

RECOGNIZING WHAT THEY NEED

Clients have needs that have to be met if they are to continue to recover and flourish. The range of such needs is wide, and you will be able to help connect them to a range of resources. You'll want to routinely be asking yourself what your client needs in the following areas:

1. **Clinical Treatments:** Do they need a specific service or intervention?

2. **Clinical Providers:** Do they need the support, or at least a review, from a specific provider or type of provider?

3. **Other Peer Support Specialists:** Would they benefit from getting to know and working with additional Peer Support Specialists?

4. **Peer Support Groups:** Do they need to be part of a peer support group of some type? Peer support groups come in a huge variety of types and formats.

5. **Other Individuals in Recovery:** Besides working with Peer Support Specialist, clients often need contact with other people in recovery.

6. **Community Social Support Opportunities:** Social support is very powerful in helping people recover. Community-based groups including religious groups, service groups, gaming and sports groups, etc., are examples of social support that clients may be open to. You'll want to have resources for the many clients you'll meet who need more support.

7. **Community-Based Social Services:** Are there community-based services that would benefit your client? You'll need to learn of the large array that is available from private agencies and state and local resources.

RECOMMENDING SERVICES

Simply recommending a service is the least likely strategy to result in your client actually connecting to another resource successfully. Recommending is just what it sounds like: You tell your client that you recommend that they do something. For example: "Given what you want to change, I recommend you start going to the weekly Depression Bipolar Association Support Group. They meet at the local Catholic church on Monday nights at 8:00 p.m."

You have made a clear recommendation; you've included your rationale for the recommendation and the specific information they will need to attend. Unfortunately, research evidence shows that many of the people receiving this type of recommendation do not follow up. That fact used to puzzle me until I thought about my own feelings about showing up at any group or activity when I don't know anyone. I anticipate that I will likely feel awkward. That image is enough to discourage me from attending. I suspect that is the case with many of our clients.

REFERRING A CLIENT TO A NEW PROVIDER OR SERVICE

Referrals can be an important opportunity for clients to get the care that they need. Many referrals don't actually result in new services, though, and can even result in the client falling out of treatment. That's why it is crucial that you do your best to ensure a successful transition. Take note of the following tips for making effective referrals.

- Clearly explain why you are suggesting a referral: What

problem will be addressed, and what is the potential benefit of the new service?

- Explain why you believe this specific provider will be helpful (for example, the experience of past clients, any special skills, special knowledge, etc.).

- Listen to the client's concerns about, or reactions to, the referral process or the specific provider, and address any questions you can. Respect their sentiments and freedom to participate in the care they desire. In most cases, if the client does not understand the referral or is resistant to entering the new service, you have more work to do.

- If possible, introduce the client and provider in person. If that is not possible, at least provide them with some written materials, including directions, schedules, descriptions of services, etc.

- After making a referral, follow up with the client to see if they attended the first meeting and engaged successfully in treatment. If not, continue your conversations about the possibility of this service.

THE WARM HANDOFF

A warm handoff involves you physically introducing your client to another provider or person. The introduction is typically done in person, though virtual warm handoffs can also be useful. You play a key role in that (1) you know each provider, (2) you are vouching for the supportiveness and skill of the other person, (3) you are recommending that your client work with the new person, and (4) you will likely maintain a relationship with the client and the other provider over time, such that if there is a problem, you can be involved in addressing it.

There is some mixed research evidence about the impact of warm handoffs, but they seem to be particularly promising when it comes to successfully engaging clients in self-help and community-based supports.

CHAPTER 22

PEER COUNSELING SUPERVISION

Peer counseling is not an easy skill to learn. It will take you years to learn to do it well, and you will need to continue to improve your technique over your career if you are to help the largest percentage of your clients.

I have heard peer counselors and even psychotherapists talk about peer counseling as a skill you are born with. Research suggests that this is not entirely true. Some people may have personality traits and natural talents that give them greater potential for being an effective peer counselor, but good peer counseling is also determined by training and the efforts over time by the peer counselor to build better and better skills.

If you are looking for a useful image for your "trade," think about the old model of training for tradespeople like carpenters and blacksmiths. They would spend years as apprentices, and then additional years as journeymen, and only after many years of learning and practicing would they be considered by the community to be masters of their trade. The certification process for Peer Support Specialists is relatively short and will put you into situations where you can start providing peer counseling with relatively little formal education and direct supervision. Do not make the mistake of thinking that you know how to provide good peer counseling because you have your certification. You are now embarking on years of learning and skill building on the road to becoming a competent and effective peer counselor.

A key to learning a complex skill is the guidance and feedback from people who already have and use the skill. In healthcare, this falls under the label of "clinical supervision."

Clinical supervisors are experienced providers who meet with you on a regular basis to review your work with you, teach you new skills, and provide you with an opportunity to consult about individual cases.

WHAT GOOD SUPERVISION LOOKS LIKE

Many people have clinical supervisors, but what does good clinical supervision look like? This is not like meeting with a work supervisor who may see you regularly in order to give you directions and to answer any work questions. Clinical supervision is a relationship that is focused on developing your peer counseling skills. It involves the *supervisee*, who wants to continue to build their skills, and the *supervisor*, who has more advanced skills and is willing and able to help the supervisee build theirs. The supervisee does not have to be early in their career either. I have known clinicians who had been practicing for thirty years who still met on a weekly basis with a more experienced clinician in an effort to continue to improve their skills.

Good clinical supervision involves a trusting supportive relationship between the peer counselor and the supervisor. Frank, open discussion is essential if the peer counselor is going to improve their skills. Trust is also important because the supervisor has to be able to point out the peer counselor's mistakes. The peer counselor needs to know that these comments are made in the service of their own improvement. These sessions often cover specific clinical cases and even specific peer counseling conversations. Some clinical supervisors request that peer counselors record audio or video of at least some peer counseling conversations and then review them during clinical supervision sessions. This can be intimidating to the peer counselor as there is no hiding mistakes when they are on tape. In a supportive clinical supervision relationship, reviewing of taped peer counseling sessions accelerates the peer counselor's development by ensuring the supervisor is able to see the peer counselor in action and can provide direct feedback on every aspect of the peer counselor's work.

FINDING A GOOD SUPERVISOR

Most organizations will provide you with some form of supervisor, but that doesn't mean that individual will provide good clinical supervision. If your work supervisor is not a skilled and seasoned peer counselor, or is not willing to provide the type of supervision that will build your skills, you may want to look for an additional clinical supervisor. Key qualifications to look for include:

1. They have more advanced skills than you, as indicated by their training and experience.

2. They understand how to provide clinical supervision and are willing to provide it to you, knowing the time commitment it will require.

3. They understand peer counseling and are willing to help you be the best peer counselor possible. They understand how peer counseling is different from other forms of

counseling and psychotherapy, and are committed to helping you provide effective peer counseling.

4.   They approach supervision in a supportive manner. There is evidence that they approach supervisees from a warm supportive stance. (Other supervisees can be sources of information about this.)

5.   While being supportive, they are also ambitious for you and so will give you direct constructive feedback. They are not afraid to point out your mistakes or to challenge you to get better.

DOES YOUR CLINICAL SUPERVISOR NEED TO BE A PEER SPECIALIST?

If you want to learn to be a good peer counselor, you want a clinical supervisor who fully understands peer counseling. In many clinical settings, experienced peer counselors may not be available or may be less available than other clinicians.

I would be cautious about having a clinical supervisor who is a psychotherapist. As we've talked about, there are important differences between peer counseling and psychotherapy. Your clinical supervisor needs to be able to help you see this clearly and develop great skills that are truly peer counseling skills. It seems unlikely that a clinician who is not a Peer Support Specialist would be able to do this effectively.

In some work settings, you may not have access to supervisors who are Peer Support Specialists and you may have to consider working with clinical supervisors from other professions. I would also consider talking with your work supervisor about your need for a more senior Peer Support Specialist and advocating for the addition of a new supervisor position.

TAKING FULL ADVANTAGE OF SUPERVISION

The benefits of clinical supervision will depend, in part, on how you approach it. I would suggest the following strategies:

1. Prepare for meetings with your clinical supervisor. Have goals for supervision: What skills do you want to improve on? Have challenging cases for review What peer counseling cases are difficult for you? What cases do you feel you could do better with? Have challenging situations that you feel you struggle with: Are there common situations across clients that you feel don't go well?

2. Talk frankly with your supervisor about what you want from the relationship. If supervision is not meeting your goals, be direct with the supervisor about that and ask what is needed to achieve those goals.

3. Be open and friendly with your supervisor. It is not uncommon to feel anxious and insecure when reviewing your work with a very skilled supervisor. Recognize that they were in supervision in the past—they know how you feel. They are not there to attack you or hurt you but rather to help you meet your professional goals. You may want to talk about any feelings of anxiety or insecurity, as that will help build your trust in your supervisor.

4. Consider using recorded sessions for review in supervision. Of course, this requires knowledge and consent of your client, but most clients are willing to give their permission if they understand why you are taping conversations and how you will protect their privacy. With recorded sessions, your supervisor will be able to give you better feedback, as they can see you providing actual peer counseling.

5. Use your supervisor as a consultant on any work- related issues that arise. Supervisors are great for getting a review of your clinical decisions. Their input on ethical issues can be wonderfully helpful. Any issues related to patient safety or your safety should be shared with them. By doing so, you are not only getting their input but protecting yourself from any second-guessing if something bad happens. For example, if you are providing peer counseling to someone who expresses suicidal ideation, your supervisor can help you think through what needs to be done to ensure that client is safe. You don't want to miss any strategy, and their experience will help ensure you don't. If something negative does happen, you may well be asked what you knew about it and what you did for the client's safety. Being able to say that you consulted with your clinical supervisor and followed their guidance will assure others that you were acting responsibly.

CHAPTER 23

STARTING TO WORK WITH
A NEW CLIENT

THE CHALLENGE
The most influential parts of most experiences are the beginning and the end. When you are starting to work with someone, the first five to ten minutes are critical. Our brains quickly draw conclusions about any new situation or new people—which is not fair, but it is a reality. We all take the limited initial information in any experience and draw conclusions about whether the situation is safe and whether there is something of potential value to us.

Given that, it is important that you think about how you will meet any new client. How will you introduce yourself? What will you say about your work? How do you want to act?

WHAT IS THE CLIENT LIKELY FEELING AND THINKING?
In a first meeting with a Peer Support Specialist, many clients will feel at least a little anxious. They are likely to have not worked

with a Peer Support Specialist before, and so they may not understand what you do and what they can expect. They will be looking to see if you are competent and trustworthy. Will they be safe with you, and if so, are they likely to get any benefit from working with you? They are also likely looking for evidence that you are personally invested in the work you are offering. If you are just doing a job to get paid, they are likely to see this and be concerned that you won't really be careful. Behind this question is the larger question of whether you care about them as a person.

A SUCCESSFUL BEGINNING

A successful start to the first meeting will provide the client a chance to meet you and see that you are both competent and safe for them. You will probably need to provide them with some basic information about yourself and your role.

In any first meeting with a new client, I always start by asking an open question about how I can be helpful. This communicates that you are clear that you are working for them and their welfare. It also gives them a chance to tell you what they might want. Some of them will not know what they want from you, and this question will help them start thinking about it. It can also help determine whether they have any unreasonable expectations for you. It is good to quickly correct such expectations.

Think about what you can say that will help your client conclude that you are competent and trustworthy. You may want to share a little about your background experience and training as a peer. If they don't understand what a Peer Support Specialist does, you may have to explain that first before you talk about your training or skill. What can you say as part of your introduction to answer the question about whether this is just a job to you and whether you actually care about the people you work with?

You may also want to talk about how you typically work as a peer counselor—what you do and what they do. This makes it clear what they can expect.

You may want to mention that it is not uncommon that, as the two of you work together, you may have some challenges in misunderstanding each other at times. You may say this as a way of conveying that you will be open and direct when you may have misunderstood them, and that you would like them to be open and direct with you if they feel there is a misunderstanding.

You'll also want to review any basic guidelines for your work. For example, you will always want to talk about the rules around privacy, documentation, and boundaries. Work with your supervisor to ensure you are covering the important initial information during your introduction. If there is anything to review about reimbursement, you should go over that as well.

KEY ISSUES TO KEEP AN EYE ON

In general, you want to be warm and friendly when you meet any new client. Many peer counselors feel anxiety when they meet new clients. While this is very understandable, you want to keep an eye on this. Your client is likely to be anxious. If you are obviously nervous, your client is likely to feel even more anxious. Even if you have to use your best relaxation exercises, you want to try to be as relaxed as you can, or at least appear relaxed.

Communicate clearly who you are and what, as a Peer Support Specialist, you can do. Explain your role to the client if it is not clear. Offer to answer any questions they may have about what you do and what they can expect from you.

Clients often think that Peer Support Specialists do not share clinical data with other clinicians. If you are part of a clinical team, their expectation can lead to unhappiness when they discover that you'll share information about them openly with the team.

Leave them with a clear idea of what your next step will be and follow through with anything you agree to do. This will be the first evidence of trustworthiness that you can provide.

CHAPTER 24

ENDING YOUR WORK WITH SOMEONE

In some peer counseling situations, there is no formal end to the counseling relationship. You may see a client for conversations over an extended period of time. It may not be clear when you will end your work together. In other situations, your work will have a formal ending set either by yourself, the client, or a program that you may work for. When there is a predictable end to the peer counseling work, you want to think about how that end will take place.

THE CHALLENGE

The way your client remembers your work together, and how they think of you, will depend on how you end your work together. This last conversation is a very important one. What makes it more challenging is that many people, including many of our clients, will not be good at saying goodbye or ending any type of relationship. For many, saying goodbye often has painful associations. For that reason, some clients may try to avoid talking openly about ending their work with you. That is unfortunate, because conversations about ending our work with clients represent a wonderful opportunity to say important things that need to be said.

WHAT IS THE CLIENT LIKELY THINKING AND FEELING?

Clients are often anxious when they meet a new peer counselor. They are often more anxious when they are going to say goodbye. They may have mixed feelings about ending your work together. They may be afraid of the next step and the fact that they won't have your support for it. They may have strong and/or confusing feelings about saying goodbye. Sometimes this is a pattern in their relationships. Other times, it is evidence that you've been important to them. Finally, they may have some lingering questions or concerns about your work together that they have not talked about.

A SUCCESSFUL ENDING

A successful conversation at the end of working together should function to pull all that you've done together in a way that provides closure.

You'll want to clearly state that this is the last time you'll meet. Some peers leave this unspoken or vague as a way to not talk about an uncomfortable topic. You don't want to avoid the reality of the ending. Say it clearly, but say it warmly.

You'll want to summarize the work you've done together. You may want to say something like, "I was just thinking back on all that we've done. We've been meeting regularly for the past X months. We've worked on Y issues (e.g., building up your friendships and getting more committed to recovery). You've made clear progress over this time. For example . . ."

You'll want to say something about what it has meant to you personally to work with this client. This is a chance to tell them about your feelings and experience and to affirm that they've had an impact on you.

You'll also want to give them a chance to share their view of the overall experience. You may want to say something like, "It is common that at the end of peer counseling, some clients have questions or even concerns about something their peer counselor said or did that they didn't understand or like. Is there anything like that which you are left with that we should talk through?" Often, they will say no, but you want to give them a chance to bring it up before it is too late.

You'll also want to review with them what their plan is going forward, particularly as it relates to the work you have done together. You may say something like, "Now going forward, we've talked about how you plan on continuing to meet with your NAMI support group and to continue in treatment with Dr. Johnson. You're also going to keep working on being more and more direct with your family."

Finally, you'll want to talk about any guidelines for them if they want to contact you in the future. You may want to remind them that they can simply contact you and how to do it. If they can't contact you directly, you should remind them to contact their other providers as needed. Again, work with your supervisor to ensure your guidance is consistent with your local guidelines.

KEY ISSUES TO KEEP AN EYE ON

Work on managing your own discomfort so that they feel permission to speak openly. Saying goodbye effectively is an important skill and is often a topic to talk about in clinical supervision.

How does your client think about the work you've done together? Is there a way to help them frame what they've accomplished? Are there any central lessons that they've learned that you can summarize and reinforce?

Like your first meeting, this last meeting is a time when they are looking to see if you care about them. Was this work meaningful to you like it was to them? You'll want to think about how to communicate your positive feelings for them and the work they did. Point out their strengths and the challenges they overcame. Point out anything you personally learned from them.

CHAPTER 25

DEALING WITH DIFFICULT PEER COUNSELING SITUATIONS

THE CLIENT IN CRISIS

We all have good and bad days. A crisis is not the same as a bad day. Someone "in a crisis" is having problems functioning because of extreme outside stressors (traumatic events, major life losses, etc.), internal stressors (hallucinations, severe depression, mania, etc.), or a combination of both. Some people can function despite huge stressors. A crisis is present when those stressors undermine the person's ability to think clearly or act in a way that is healthy.

Some people in crisis may be suicidal. Others may be immobilized so that they can't adequately take care of themselves or ask for help. Because of the impact on their functioning, people in a crisis often need extra effort and help from others.

If you are working with someone and they go into a crisis, you will want to take a few key steps:

- **Address Any Safety Concerns:** Review and follow the procedures for your organization regarding patient safety. Talk with your supervisor, team members, and possibly other Peer Support Specialists to ensure you are recognizing and addressing all safety concerns. Appendix A includes some core strategies for addressing common safety issues.

- **Draw In Additional Help:** Besides your supervisor, there will likely be other clinicians on your team with more experience working with clients in crisis. You will want to draw them into helping your client. They will be able to evaluate the client for additional clinical needs such as medication, diversion services, or hospitalization.

- **Continue to Support Your Client:** Crises are frightening to the person living through them. They often don't know what is happening and fear that their life is falling apart in a way that they don't understand. Peer counselors can play a valuable role by continuing to provide support during and after the crisis. Know that they will be wondering what is happening to them and what is going to happen to them in the future. If you have personal experience with crises or hospitalization, you may have an opportunity to share that as part of a recovery story. Your client will likely benefit from reassurance that a crisis is not uncommon and they will recover. They may also benefit from some discussion about what is coming next. Again, collaborate closely with the rest of your clinical team and your supervisor in these situations.

THE CLIENT IS SOMEONE YOU HAVE ANOTHER RELATIONSHIP WITH

Ethics codes say you should try to avoid dual relationships, such as providing services to a friend, coworker, or relative, as this often leads to confusion as to your role and motives. This is not always possible, particularly in areas with few Peer Support Specialists or few healthcare providers.

If you can avoid it, do so by refusing to work with clients whom you have an existing relationship with, and avoid developing any other relationships with people who are your clients. If you find yourself in a dual relationship, consider whether you can refer your client to someone else. Talk with your supervisor about a strategy for dealing with the situation.

If you can't avoid it:
1. Be clear on the challenge.
2. Be clear about each role.
3. Be clear on what you will do if the dual relationship creates a conflict.
4. Talk with a supervisor or peer mentor.
5. Document what you have done to manage this ethically.

THE CLIENT WANTS TO TELL YOU A SECRET

You may encounter a situation in which the client wants to tell you something they don't want shared with other clinicians. What is the problem? This breaks the agreement you have with the other clinicians. Hopefully you have told this and every client at the outset that you are part of a team and will not keep secrets. Telling them directly is particularly important because many clients have issues with trust. They may not trust others on your team. Some clients also have a pattern of creating conflict between people—they do this at home, and they do it in clinical settings.

If they raise the possibility of sharing something confidential, remind them of what you told them at the start of peer counseling. You also want to explain how secrets between members of their clinical team are not good for them and their care. Use this as an opportunity for education about good communication and healthy boundaries.

Be assertive. Clients can be convincing about why you should bend your own guidelines. If you are in doubt about what to do, talk with your supervisor. I often find that another person's perspective makes it easier to see what to do. Even thinking about how a supervisor will respond can help you see the best strategy to take.

THE CLIENT DOES NOT WANT TO WORK WITH YOU ANY LONGER

I am assuming that this work is personal for you—you have personal motivations for wanting to provide peer counseling to help others. It can be painful if a client no longer wants to work with you and can feel like rejection or a statement about your competence. Fortunately, all clinicians have this experience. You are not going to be helpful to every client. The client-peer counselor mix depends on so many things, including personality and style. It is not uncommon that a combination does not work for the client.

Always remind yourself that your client has the right to choose services and providers. As a Peer Support Specialist, you should always be advocating for their right to manage their own healthcare, including whether they want to participate in peer counseling and whether they want to work with you.

Regardless of why they want to stop working with you, you should support their decision. Be professional. In most situations, you'll want to ask about why they want to stop. This conversation should give you some important information. It may be that you've made some mistakes and their feedback will help you improve your work. It could be that their mental health concern is driving the decision, and so their explanation can help you see this. You might even be able to help them think more clearly about their decision. What you don't want to do is to actively fight their decision to end peer counseling.

YOU DON'T WANT TO WORK WITH THE CLIENT

You will have clients that you don't want to work with. It could be something about them or about the chemistry, but you are left feeling that you just don't want to work with them.

As a peer counselor, you want to always be careful to understand these situations, and to learn as much as you can from them. Talking with a clinical supervisor can help you consider (1) what about the client is causing you to feel this way, (2) what about you may be contributing to this feeling, and (3) how best to proceed.

If you feel that it is best to stop working with your client, and your supervisor understands and supports your decision, you will want to move toward ending the peer counseling relationship. Some peer counselors don't feel that they have the right to end a peer counseling relationship and that they always have to do what the client wants. This is clearly not true—you have the right to make decisions about your work (National Association of Peer Supporters, 2019). The key is how to explain this to your client in a way that is not hurtful and to help them find another peer counselor or other needed support.

If you think the client will benefit from hearing about the specifics of why you don't want to work with them, you may consider sharing those. It is more likely that you'll want to say something like, "After working together for this time, I've been feeling like I'm not the right person to help. I've talked with my supervisor about this and they agree that there are likely other people who could be more helpful. I have some referrals of people I think will be helpful."

The client may react in a wide range of ways. Often, they also feel that a change is needed and so they may respond more positively than you anticipate. If they respond by being upset or demanding that you not stop working together, you'll want to listen and be supportive, while being firm about your decision. Again, I find it helpful in these situations to draw in my supervisor.

OTHER CLINICIANS HAVE CONCERNS ABOUT YOU WORKING WITH A CLIENT

Most Peer Support Specialists work on a team of clinicians. From time to time, clinicians on the team may have concerns about you working with a particular client. There can be many reasons for these concerns. They may know the client well and have concerns about whether peer counseling will be helpful. Or they may not understand peer counseling.

You should try to talk openly and nondefensively with them about their concerns. You want to understand their reasoning. Keep your focus on the welfare of your client, and try to avoid taking their concerns as an affront to you. You are both on the same team, and your shared concern about the recovery of your client must be the top priority.

Again, consider talking with your supervisor about this situation. If appropriate, consider asking your supervisor to join the meeting with the other provider to help manage the discussion.

THE CLIENT DISAPPEARS

You may have a client who just stops meeting with you. They don't communicate that they are stopping and give no explanation.

This can be the client's way of ending the peer counseling. It can also be evidence of a relapse or some other negative event.

It is important for there to be some form of closure to any peer counseling relationship. In most cases, you will want to try to contact the client and ask to talk with them. You will want to remind them they have the right to stop and that you are fully supportive of their decision, but that you'd like to talk with them about it. Try to find out if the client does want to end the peer counseling and have a conversation about why. If this is the end, try to tie up any loose ends and create a positive goodbye.

Some clients are difficult to reach. You may have a concern about the safety of a client who has disappeared. You'll want to talk about the best response with your supervisor and your clinical team. If your client is safe and has just "ghosted" you as a way to end peer counseling, you have limited options besides offering them an opportunity to talk.

Your own reaction is very important. When clients abruptly end peer counseling, you'll hopefully be curious as to why and whether there is anything for you to learn. You'll also want to remind yourself that this happens to all clinicians and doesn't necessarily mean anything specific about you. It is more likely to be evidence of something about the client. Talk openly with your supervisor and/or mentor about your reaction.

THE CLIENT CONFUSES YOU WITH A PSYCHOTHERAPIST

We often overestimate how much our clients understand about the different providers and services they are using. This is particularly true when it comes to peer support.

We've talked previously about the important differences between peer counseling and psychotherapy. Your clients are not likely to understand this difference. It is important that you be very clear with them about the difference, and watch for situations in which they are confused about the two.

If you find your client is drawing you into peer counseling that looks more like psychotherapy, you'll want to talk with them about that. Remind them of the differences and what you provide as a peer counselor. Remind them of your training and what your role is. Offer to provide them a referral to a psychotherapist if they do not have one. If they do have one, you want to help them understand the difference between what you can provide and what they should get from their therapist.

In the end, it is your responsibility to ensure that you are providing peer counseling. If your client continues to get this confused, it will still be your responsibility to stay true to your role.

THE CLIENT IS RELAPSING

Relapses are common in most mental health conditions, and so are likely to happen to some clients while you are working with them. You'll want to consider the following issues related to relapse and bring them up with your team and your supervisor.

1. Does the team know about the relapse? If not, share openly what you know.

2. Are there any safety concerns arising because of the relapse? If so, respond quickly to ensure everything that can be done to appropriately support those safety issues is being done. Again, this is a situation to immediately talk about with your supervisor.

3. Are there additional services or supports that your client needs to help them address the relapse? Be ready to make referrals and provide warm handoffs to whatever they need.

Clients often have strong reactions to relapses. As a peer counselor, you can have a key role in helping them understand what is happening and drawing reasonable conclusions about what a relapse means. Some clients try to flee from clinical care and peer support when they relapse. As a Peer Support Specialist, you can help them maintain their connection to you and the rest of their providers.

Relapses can have a negative impact on hope—be ready to address this directly, helping your client understand that relapses are common and a natural part of recovery. Perhaps you have a good recovery story about relapses that you can share or can introduce them to another Peer Support Specialist who does.

Some relapses have good lessons for recovery. Help your client see that there are some positive opportunities for learning in a relapse. Help them be curious about what contributed to their relapse and what this may mean for their recovery as they move forward.

A relapse is a common event, but it can be both very dangerous to a client's progress in recovery and an opportunity for learning that promotes further recovery. You want to be watchful and respond quickly to relapses in a way that supports a positive outcome.

THE CLIENT SETS UP CONFLICT BETWEEN YOU AND OTHER CLINICIANS

Occasionally you may have clients who have clinical problems that are associated with longstanding patterns of conflict with others. Sometimes it is the client who is in conflict. Sometimes it is the client who encourages conflict between other people.

While it is fairly rare, you may have a client who will act in a way that encourages conflict between members of your clinical team. This is a challenging situation for teams, as these clients are often very indirect and subtle in how they do this. You want to work with your supervisor to recognize and address it.

As part of being a good peer counselor, you should always be watching your behavior and that of your team. If you notice a lot of conflict in your team related to a specific client, conflict that is not typical for your team, you should be curious as to what is driving it. Again, talk with your supervisor about whether there is any link to a specific client and whether this is reflective of their mental health condition.

Responding carefully and slowly when this type of conflict arises will mean the difference between being helpful to your client and allowing lasting damage to your team while not helping the client.

CHAPTER 26

DEALING WITH CHALLENGING CLIENTS

THE CLIENT WHO DOESN'T TALK

Some clients don't talk very much in peer counseling, which is a challenge, given the importance of talking. Plus, it can feel awkward for you as the peer counselor.

A client who doesn't talk may be struggling in a number of different ways. You will need to determine what their quietness means.

Is it evidence that they have not yet learned to trust you? It is only reasonable that new clients will be concerned about whether you are trustworthy. Some will respond by being very guarded at first. They remain quiet until they can tell whether you are competent and care about them. This concern should subside over the first few conversations, as they get to know that you are trustworthy. If it does not, then there is a different explanation.

Is it evidence that the client does not want to be in peer counseling? Is it a passive way to avoid dealing with a problem? If so, you'll want to address the issue and ask what they want to do. You don't want to provide peer counseling to anyone who does not want it.

Is it evidence of their ambivalence about being in peer counseling? Everyone is ambivalent to some degree about peer counseling and treatment in general. If the ambivalence is so strong that they are not talking, you'll want to focus on that ambivalence. Try to help them think and maybe talk about why they might be ambivalent. What might they be afraid of? Have they had bad experiences in the past?

Is it evidence that they are not used to talking and don't know what to do? Some people don't connect with others by talking and may prefer doing things with them or another way of connecting. Such individuals usually feel uneasy talking about themselves or talking openly. If not talking is a longstanding pattern for this client, you'll want to recognize and accept that peer counseling will be a challenging process for them. It can still be very helpful, but it will require that they develop new skills of talking openly. You may want to consider doing something together while you are talking. For example, would it help to take a walk with them while you are talking? Is there a different activity you could add to help them be more comfortable? You'll want to be patient and supportive in this situation.

Is it evidence that the client is trying to get you to lead the discussion? Some clients don't want to lead the conversation in peer counseling, and if the client is quiet enough, some peer counselors will fill in the silence and will actually take the lead in the session. This is rarely helpful over time. Clients need to take at least some leadership of their own peer counseling sessions. For those who seem resistant to doing so, you'll want to point that out to them, and inquire about why they may struggle in leading the discussion. Help them see that without them identifying goals for the peer counseling and bringing in information about their lives and experiences, the peer counseling is not going to be helpful.

THE CLIENT WHO TALKS AND TALKS BUT DOES NOT APPEAR TO SAY ANYTHING IMPORTANT

You are likely to run across a few clients who are quite talkative but never seem to say anything substantive. They may chat about lots of topics, and even talk so much that you have trouble getting a word in. The problem is that they are not talking openly about any issues they want to work on. They are not talking about genuine feelings or thoughts, and their conversation doesn't seem to reflect any goal.

This may be a strategy by the client to avoid uncomfortable conversations by filling the time with safe talk. Look for why they may not feel safe talking about themselves. You may want to ask about this specifically. If they cannot talk about it directly, you may want to try to patiently see if they do better as they learn to trust you. I tend to reward these clients when they make any comments that do share something personal or that focus on a problem. I do that by saying something like, "I'm really glad you said that. Tell me more about that." Or "That comment is very helpful. What else do you think about that?"

If the client continues to avoid meaningful conversation over several peer counseling sessions, you'll want to consider whether they can really benefit from peer counseling. You can raise this with them, and even suggest ending if you feel it is clear that they are not going to be able to use your help.

THE CLIENT WHO TALKS AND TALKS BUT NEVER ACTS

This client may sound similar to the previous one, but there is a key difference. This client talks about meaningful issues and may even be very open about their feelings and goals. What they don't do is actually act on anything they or you say in the peer counseling. Without any follow-through, it is unclear whether the peer counseling is really having any benefit.

You'll want to help the client see the disconnect between what they say and what they do. Help them explore why their actions are not matching their words. At times, we all have trouble following through on what we want to do, but when this is a general pattern for a client, it is worth talking openly about it repeatedly until the client finds a way to better connect their thoughts and actions.

THE CLIENT WHO DISAGREES WITH EVERYTHING YOU SAY

On occasion you may have a client who openly disagrees with everything you say. You want clients to disagree with you when they really don't agree, but when it is a consistent pattern for them, then something else is going on.

The most common explanation is that the client is, again, simply uncomfortable with the peer counseling situation and feels anxious about another person hearing about their life. Disagreeing with people can be a good way to push people away, and to remind others that the client is ultimately in control.

If this is about trust, you know how to deal with that. By being trustworthy and patient, most clients will come to trust you and these behaviors will become less and less common. If they don't, then you may want to bring it up with your client. You could say something like, "Would it be OK if I bring up something I've noticed about our conversations? Compared to most clients I've worked with; you seem to disagree with me on almost anything I say. What do you think that may mean?"

If the pattern continues and the client cannot talk openly about it, you need to consider whether they are actually benefiting from the peer counseling. If they are, you may just need to tolerate the disagreements in the service of their recovery. If they are not benefiting, you should consider whether ending the peer counseling would be appropriate. I would encourage you to talk with your supervisor before making a decision in a situation like this.

THE CLIENT WHO AGREES WITH EVERYTHING YOU SAY

The opposite of the last scenario is the client who agrees with everything you say. This is also a problem. It is great when you are listening so well that clients agree with many of your comments, but you will never have a client who genuinely agrees with everything. When a client has this pattern, something else is going on that you want to understand and address.

I would suggest that you always assume that you are getting something wrong at least 10 percent of the time, and so you should expect your client to correct you at least that often. When that is not happening, it is reasonable to conclude that you are wrong and they are purposefully acting as though you are right. Are they afraid of correcting you? Are they concerned that something bad will happen if they disagree with you? Do they think you will get angry or hurt? Do they think you will stop being the peer counselor?

You want to get curious about what is behind this behavior, and then help the client get curious. You might say something like, "I notice that you agree with me whenever I make any comment.

I'm not used to that—I am never always right and most of my clients disagree with me at least some of the time. What do you think that may mean?" You might also say something like, "I've noticed that you almost never disagree with me on anything. What do you think would happen if you did?"

THE CLIENT WITH POOR BOUNDARIES

Boundaries are valuable psychological structures that help us manage our lives successfully. Some of your clients will have difficulties with the concept of boundaries—that is often part of the reason they are receiving clinical help. They may not have a clear sense of appropriate boundaries between themselves and you as a Peer Support Specialist. They may start to treat you as a friend or potential love interest. They may ask to socialize with you outside of your job or to borrow money from you. They may try to build a relationship with you on social media.

The concept of boundaries is a valuable tool in recovery. Some mental illnesses are specifically associated with problems with interpersonal boundaries. When you see clients struggle with boundaries, you will want use this as an opportunity to educate them about the value and function of psychological boundaries. This will help you see whether they simply don't know that they are supposed to attend to boundaries in peer counseling or even in other parts of their life.

If they understand the concept but still try to break the boundary in your role as peer counselor, that is a more concerning situation. You will want to talk openly with your clinical team and your supervisor about any boundary crossings or client behavior that moves toward a breach of boundaries.

It is important that you not participate in any boundary crossing, and it is critical for you to understand and consistently maintain appropriate boundaries with all clients in every situation. Because of the damage to clients' trust in the healthcare or social service organization, inappropriate boundary crossings with clients often result in disciplinary action or termination for the employee.

It is never appropriate to engage in sexual acts with a client. Anytime romantic feelings arise between you and a client, you should seek consultation and help.

THE CLIENT WHO IS A FUZZY THINKER

Some clients will be very clear thinkers, able to describe problems, logical solutions, and the resulting outcomes. You will also likely become clearer and clearer in your own thinking as you develop as a peer counselor. Good peer work, just like all good clinical work, starts with a client's goal for a change they want to make, then looks for possible strategies for making the change, then identifies the most promising strategy, followed by a trial of the strategy and an evaluation of the outcome.

Some clients will be particularly poor at clear thinking. They may have trouble thinking or talking logically about problems or solutions. This is typically a longstanding pattern evident in other parts of their life. They may talk in the peer counseling sessions in ways that seem to be circular or chaotic. You may feel a sense of confusion or hopelessness when a client has trouble thinking clearly about how to solve a problem.

As a peer counselor, you can help bring clearer problem-solving into the session for this type of client. They may need to rely on you to organize their thoughts or their efforts. Be careful not to take over the conversation, though; it still needs to reflect their concerns and desires. But it can be useful if you help them set clear goals and review the outcomes of their efforts to change.

THE CLIENT WHO COMPETES WITH YOU

You may come across clients who appear to feel that they need to compete with you. They may make comments about how they are better than you in some way. They may be similar to the client who always disagrees with you, but this is usually in the service of communicating that they know more than you or do things better than you.

This can be quite annoying for the peer counselor. You may want try to reframe this as a sign that your client is struggling. You want to become curious about why they feel a need to compete with you.

Some people see life as a continuous competition and that they are competing with everyone, so they are simply treating you like they treat everyone. That is an exhausting approach to life and may be very connected to the problems they are working on. You want to help them see what they are doing and its cost.

Some clients don't generally feel competitive with everyone, just with you. There may be something about the peer counselor role that makes them feel they have to prove they know more than you or that they don't need your help. Again, you want to become curious about what they are feeling and help them become curious too. Competing with you is a waste of their peer counseling time, and so helping them see what is behind their behavior should help them stop it.

THE CLIENT WHO MAKES YOU FEEL UNCOMFORTABLE BUT YOU DON'T KNOW WHY

On a rare occasion, you'll have a client that you feel uncomfortable with, but you can't figure out why. You may have a vague feeling that you are missing something important and that there is some risk to the client or to the peer counseling.

This is an important situation that you want to take seriously. You may be picking up on something essential that you do not understand or can't put into words easily. In these situations, you will want to talk with a supervisor and get their input. Look for more information to see if that fills in an important gap in your knowledge. You may also consult with respected colleagues to get their input. You will also want to document your efforts, including any evaluations or efforts to address safety.

CHAPTER 27

ETHICAL ISSUES

Legal and ethical rules apply to healthcare settings and to interactions between staff and patients, including between peer counselors and their clients. To avoid legal and ethical problems, it is important to be aware of basic principles and to know where to get advice when issues arise. Recognize that these questions *will* arise in your work and are often more complex to solve than you might anticipate.

To adequately prepare yourself, take the following precautions:

- **Know the Basic Rules That Govern Your Role in Your Organization.** Talk with your supervisor and coworkers about the rules to ensure that everyone understands and is complying with them. Be outspoken about any need to modify or clarify the rules when necessary, and any need for additional education or information.

- **Talk About Legal and Ethical Issues on a Regular Basis with Your Supervisor and Coworkers.** The more you talk about these issues, the more prepared you will be to recognize and deal with them.

- **Know What Resources Are Available to You as a Peer and as an Employee.** Be aware of policies, trainings, and committees that can help you, so you know where to turn when legal or ethical questions arise.

KEY ETHICAL ISSUES IN PEER COUNSELING

The following issues should guide your practice as a peer counselor:

1. **The Agenda for Your Work.** Peer counseling is done for the benefit of the client. Your actions should reflect that the welfare of the client is your top priority, even when the client is difficult to work with.

2. **Conflict of Interest.** You avoid any situation in which you have, or could appear to have, a conflict of interest related to your role as a peer counselor.

3. **Multiple Roles.** Similarly, you avoid any situation in which you have or could appear to have multiple roles with your client. You do not start peer counseling with someone with whom you have an existing relationship that would compromise your role as a peer counselor. You do not provide formal peer counseling to family members, friends, or people you know from other settings.

4. **Boundaries.** You maintain professional boundaries around your work as a peer counselor. You do not

engage in unprofessional behavior and you don't cross professional boundaries with clients.

5. **Sexual Relationships.** It is always unethical to have a sexual relationship with anyone you are providing peer counseling to, or whom you have previously provided peer counseling to if the period of time since you provided support is short enough that you or others would consider it likely that you have taken advantage of your past relationship with your client. You will want to talk about any possible issues of this type with your supervisor.

6. **Financial Relationships.** It is almost always unethical to enter into a separate business relationship with anyone you are providing peer counseling to, or that you have previously provided counseling to if the period of time since you provided support is short enough that you or others would consider it likely that you have taken advantage of your past relationship with your client. For example, you should not employ clients to do work for you or sell things to them from a different business. Gifts from and to your clients are areas of ethical concern and should not be of more than nominal value. You will want to know the specific guidelines of your organization in this area.

7. **Privacy.** Clients have the right to privacy, including privacy around information they share as part of their peer counseling. You should not share information you learn from clients with people outside your clinical team. When you do share with your clinical team, it should only be in the context of helping the client and getting feedback on your work in order to improve your skills and support.

There are some important exceptions to this. You may need to share information as part of the basic business operations of your organization (e.g., date of appointment, service provided, problem addressed). In situations where you have information about risk to the safety of your client or other identifiable people, you are obligated as a peer support specialist to take action to attempt to preserve that safety. That would include taking action to protect a suicidal client or to protect others from a client who tells you about child abuse, elder abuse, or abuse of a disabled person. Work with your supervisor to ensure you understand the privacy guidelines at your organization.

8. **The Right to Informed Consent.** Clients have the right to understand what services they are going to receive and what the risks and benefits are of those services. They have the right to decline any services and to stop any services they no longer want. They have the right to request a change of providers, including of peer counselors.

9. **Coercion.** Clients have the right to receive healthcare that is free of coercion. Your responsibility can include providing them with information and even recommendations about their care or their actions, but you should not take actions that the client or others may see as coercion.

COMMON PEER ETHICAL GUIDELINES

As a Peer Support Specialist, you must work in accordance with the ethical guidelines established by your organization and the medical community at large. Be sure that you know them and that you participate in any training offered to you about ethical guidelines for your work.

Here is a list of common ethical guidelines for Peer Support Specialists to know.

- Maintain high standards of personal conduct.

- Support the self-determination of the clients you work with.

- Support clients' full integration into their chosen communities.

- Serve as a role model of recovery for others.

- Openly share your recovery stories when appropriate.

- Respect the rights and dignity of all clients, including their right to privacy and confidentiality.

- Respect individual and cultural differences.

- Never practice or condone any form of discrimination.

- Never intimidate, threaten, harass, or use excessive influence, physical force, or verbal abuse against clients.

- Never engage in sexual or intimate activities with clients.

- Do not exchange gifts of significant value with clients.

- Continue to pursue recovery in your own life.

CHAPTER 28

CULTURAL COMPETENCE AND CULTURAL HUMILITY

In the context of a healthcare setting, *cultural competence* is defined as "the ability of providers and organizations to effectively deliver healthcare services that meet the social, cultural, and linguistic needs of patients" (Georgetown, 2024). Culturally competent peer counseling involves delivering peer counseling in a way that successfully meets the client's needs in these areas such that background factors do not limit or undermine the positive impact of the peer counseling.

We've already talked about the importance of respecting individual differences in peer counseling in chapter 2. To be effective, though, the peer counselor has to do more than respect the variations between clients. They need to have at least a basic understanding of how those variables impact the client's and the peer counselor's ability to participate in peer counseling.

There are many dimensions of cultures and subcultures that can help you better understand some of your clients. I've tried to address some of the more common dimensions, but they are certainly not the only ones.

RACE AND ETHNICITY

The relationship between healthcare organizations and racial/ethnic subgroups in the US is a complicated one. The large amount of research on this topic suggests that racial and ethnic minorities are typically less likely to participate in healthcare fully and are at higher risk for dropping out of services before they gain the targeted benefit (Artiga, Orgera & Pham, 2020). This is true of African Americans (Henderson et al., 2015), Asian Americans (Yang, Rodgers, Lee & Lê Cook, 2020), Hispanic Americans (Bridges, de Arellano, Rheingold, Danielson & Silcott, 2010), Native Americans and Alaskan Natives (Jones, 2006), and Native Hawaiians and Pacific Islanders (Galinsky, Zelaya, Barnes & Simile, 2022).

The nature of barriers to participation in treatment varies between groups. For example, Asian Americans are less likely to see themselves as needing mental healthcare than white non-Hispanic adults, and so are less likely to seek help (Yang, Rodgers, Lee & Lê Cook, 2020). African Americans are more likely to distrust providers and to feel the effects of stigma related to mental illness (Evans-Lacko, Henderson & Thornicroft, 2013). Depending on the clients you serve, you'll want to learn as much as you can about patterns in how they see healthcare, mental health, and recovery, and use that information to successfully build your peer counseling relationship with those clients.

GENDER, SEXUAL ORIENTATION, AND GENDER IDENTITY

Sexual orientation refers to the emotional, romantic, or sexual attraction to another person. *Gender identity* is a person's perception of themselves as a man or woman. There are dramatic differences in the rates of various mental illnesses between men and women. Different illnesses can even look different in men and women. Gender is also related to significant differences in how willing people are to ask for help and the risk that they will drop out once they do get help.

It is not surprising then that many clients will have clear preferences in terms of the gender of any Peer Support Specialists that they will work with. This is quite reasonable, and so you will want to attend to those preferences and abide by them. When you do work with clients who are different from you in terms of gender, be alert to ways that this difference impacts the peer counseling and your client's experience. You will want to be open to talking about this with clients.

The acronym LGBTQ combines references to sexual orientation with gender identity. LGBTQ populations are more likely to experience mental health symptoms—primarily depression, suicidal ideation, and suicidal behaviors (Mustanski, Garofalo & Emerson, 2010). Unfortunately, they are more likely to have concerns that healthcare clinicians may not understand their experience and may not provide good care for them. There have been efforts to develop specialty mental health teams for this population. You may want to form contacts with LGBTQ Peer Support Specialists who work primarily with this group and to consider referring to specialty LGBTQ services when available.

AGE

Age is relevant to your clients in several ways. Physical age is a risk factor for different mental illnesses, medical illnesses, and life problems. Being alert to age-related risk factors and life challenges will help you anticipate problems your clients may face. Age is also related to general patterns in functioning. For example, as adults age, they develop better skills at managing emotion and are more likely to have high life satisfaction. Younger adults are more likely to report mental health concerns that they are not receiving treatment for, and when they do enter treatment, they are more likely to drop out early. Health problems, marital problems, work problems, and social isolation all vary with age. You'll want to be aware of the age of and aging issues for each of your clients.

EDUCATION AND INTELLIGENCE

Education and intelligence are closely related in most people. The more education someone has completed, the brighter they are likely to be. That is not always the case, as some life situations make it hard for bright people to pursue education.

Higher levels of education and intelligence are associated with better participation in mental healthcare. Having a college education or higher is associated with a higher likelihood of recognizing a mental healthcare need and using needed mental healthcare (Olsson, Hensing, Burström & Löve, 2021). Once in care, people with a college education or higher are less likely to drop out. Mental healthcare and recovery can be complex and so it would make sense that brighter, better-educated clients are more likely to successfully navigate those services.

FINANCIAL RESOURCES AND BACKGROUND

Income and overall financial resources are related to having health insurance, and insurance is directly related to use of mental health services (Walker, Cummings, Hockenberry & Druss, 2015). It appears that the perception of need and the willingness to participate in care is a larger predictor of use than having resources for treatment (Steele, Dewa & Lee, 2007). For example, in a large study of college students who had access to full healthcare resources, most of those who needed mental healthcare did not access it. When asked why, most said they did not see a need for or were unaware of services. Even when financial resources for care were controlled, having a lower socioeconomic background was still predictive of not seeking care (Eisenberg, Gollust, Golberstein & Hefner, 2007).

RURAL VS. URBAN/SUBURBAN

Rural areas of the US are less likely to have mental health specialty services available, and when they do, they tend to be less up-to-date and of lesser quality. It is not surprising then that rural adults are less likely to recognize a need for mental healthcare, less likely to enter treatment, and when they do enter, they are more likely to drop out (Hauenstein et al., 2006). This points to an opportunity for peer support services to help rural clients better utilize those services. Peer support and peer counseling has been identified as one of the key strategies for addressing the gap in mental healthcare experienced by rural adults.

One of the key differences between people living in rural versus urban/suburban areas in the US is their core values. In particular, rural adults are more likely to place a high value on self-reliance and independence (Fischer et al., 2016). This makes sense, given the nature of agricultural work and the lack of resources in those regions. For peer counseling, that high value on self-reliance may mean that your client is less likely to speak up when they have a need, and less likely to engage in needed clinical services. Again, Peer Support Specialists have a potential role in helping clients think through their view of self-reliance, and to seek out help when it is appropriate.

RELIGION AND SPIRITUALITY

A great deal of variation exists between people in terms of religious values, religious behavior, and their view of spirituality. Research suggests that many mental health clients value religion and/or spirituality and would like to be able to talk about it as part of their recovery. Research also suggests that most traditional mental health professionals (psychiatrists, psychologists, social workers, etc.) have little formal training in working with religion and/or spirituality and are less likely to value religion than their clients. This creates a gap between what clients want and what clinicians are trained to provide. Peer counseling can be a place where this gap is talked about. Be alert to these issues, as well as your own views and values on religion and spirituality. Look for training opportunities to build your skills to talk about this topic with your clients in a helpful way.

SOCIAL CONNECTION

Your clients will differ greatly in the degree to which they have social support. They will also differ in their preference for social connection. There is currently a great deal of interest in social isolation and loneliness, which has been steadily growing on average in people living in the US.

Social isolation is defined as having low social support. Some people actually prefer low social connection and so do not report feeling unhappy with low levels of social support. *Loneliness* can be defined as subjective social isolation. Both social isolation and loneliness are associated with higher health and mental health concerns and shorter lifespans (Byhoff et al., 2022; Holt-Lunstad, Smith, Baker, Harris & Stephenson, 2015), indicating that we should be concerned about clients who are (1) lonely regardless of their degree of social support, and (2) isolated regardless of whether they feel lonely.

There is some evidence that some clients use healthcare as a substitute for social support (Cruwys, Wakefield, Sani, Dingle & Jetten, 2018). As a Peer Support Specialist, you may be able to identify this situation more easily than others. Peer counseling can be a good setting for clients to work on addressing isolation and/or loneliness by building real social connection in the community.

Each of your clients has a combination of background factors, current factors, and future potentials. With experience, you will gain greater insight into patterns within and between people. These patterns will guide your efforts to help your clients make good treatment and peer support decisions for themselves and for those around them.

CULTURAL HUMILITY

The term *cultural humility* is increasingly seen as a valuable stance for any provider of mental health services. Cultural humility has been defined as "a lifelong process of self-reflection and self-critique whereby the individual not only learns about another's culture, but one starts with an examination of her/his own beliefs and cultural identities" (Tervalon & Murray-Garcia, 1998).

The focus on "humility" reflects the reality that people, and various groups of people, differ in many ways—some of which we are aware of and some of which we don't see. At the same time, we as individuals and as members of many groups also have different ways of seeing life and other people. We are hopefully aware of some of these filters in our perspective, but we certainly are unaware of others. If we want to accurately understand our clients, we need a stance of "cultural humility" that involves an acceptance that we don't fully understand others and we don't fully understand some of the blinders on our own eyes. Given the great variations between your clients, a stance of cultural humility seems to be not only appropriate but of great value in helping you continue to be a better and more effective peer counselor.

CHAPTER 29

ADVANCING YOUR SKILLS

As we have discussed, peer counseling is a complex skill that takes years of hard work to master. You will never know all that you need to know to be helpful to every client. You will never have all the skills and mastery you will need. For this reason, I encourage all peer counselors, and all clinicians, to consider themselves as perpetual students of their craft. You always want to be seeking more knowledge and more training, and looking at how to include the newest knowledge into your work. Consider a few key strategies.

EDUCATION

There are organizations whose sole mission is to generate and disseminate the latest information about how to provide effective help to people with clinical problems. Each field has people paid to do research to improve treatment. That information is then collected by others who are paid to educate providers. This training has traditionally been in-person in the form of lectures, seminars, and educational retreats. Increasingly these trainings are available via web-based seminars and recorded lectures.

Your organization likely has trainings that are designed for you. Take advantage of any you think will be helpful. You'll also want to consider what training you need that they are not providing, and independently seek that out.

You may want to consider going to a local or national conference or convention. These are often rich opportunities to receive the most current training and education. Peer Support Specialists may want to consider the annual meetings of the National Alliance on Mental Illness (NAMI; www.NAMI.org/Support-Education), the National Association of Peer Supporters (NAPS; www.peersupportworks.org), or Mental Health America (MHA; https://mhanational.org).

SUPERVISION

Ongoing clinical supervision with a skilled seasoned provider who knows and understands peer counseling may be your best bet for developing truly advanced skills. See chapter 22 for more details.

BOOKS AND ARTICLES

A wide range of books related to peer support and peer counseling are available. Some of these have been written for peer counseling in other settings such as schools and colleges. Books about basic peer counseling skills can be very useful, as well as books and training materials related to psychotherapy. As we discussed in chapter 1, there are important differences between peer counseling and psychotherapy. These resources may be useful to you as long as you are careful to take the information that is relevant to peer counseling but leave the information that is specific to psychotherapy.

There is a growing body of literature about peer support and peer counseling in the professional databases. If you query "peer counseling" on Google Scholar, you'll find over thirty thousand articles on this topic. Some will be highly technical and not particularly helpful. Others will be very useful and relevant.

YOUR OWN COUNSELING

You may want to consider whether you would be willing to participate in peer counseling or even psychotherapy as a client in order to build your peer counseling skills. The experience of receiving counseling is a great learning experience. The increased self-awareness that you are likely to gain will also be a great help in building your peer counseling skills. This type of direct experiential learning can have a major impact on your ability to help others. You may want to talk with your peers and supervisor about this possibility.

PEER COUNSELING AS A CAREER

Peer counseling is a valuable part of the recovery supports that people need to navigate the challenges of healthcare in a way that allows them to rebuild their lives. If you pursue this vocation over time, you'll benefit a large number of people who need support. You'll also use your own experiences, some of which may have been quite painful for you at the time, to help others build new lives. Your pain may be what helps them. Finally, the pursuit of being an effective peer counselor will help you build greater skills in your own recovery and greater wisdom about the challenges we all face in building a meaningful life.

APPENDIX A: DEALING WITH CRITICAL SITUATIONS

As a Peer Support Specialist, you will be in situations where you may have to respond to a range of high-risk challenges. Knowing how to respond effectively is essential for all Peer Support Specialists, regardless of where you work and what your particular focus might be.

BROAD STRATEGIES

- Be alert and watchful. Know what you are looking for and consistently keep an eye out for it.

- Learn and follow the local guidelines for emergency responses at your organization. Talk about them with your supervisor so you are clear on all procedures before emergencies happen.

- Practice response procedures so you know them fully. Practice and preparation before an incident will ensure that you know how to respond well when a true emergency arises, and that you can do so while under stress.

- Alert others immediately when you find yourself in an emergency situation. Activate safety alert systems and notify supervisors and other coworkers. Clinical providers have special training in dealing with clinical emergencies. Get them involved quickly and let them take the lead.

- Try to stay calm. Your ability to think clearly in an emergency will be critical for following through with an effective response.

- "First things first": If you see someone in a critical situation, that becomes your top priority. Do not continue to work on other peer counseling topics when you see someone in a critical situation – address the situation first. Attend to immediate safety needs for yourself and those around you before placing all your attention elsewhere.

MAKING A 911 CALL

- Tell the operator what and where the emergency is.
- If someone is injured, tell the operator who is injured and the nature of the injury.

- If there are ongoing dangers in the area that could affect the responders, describe these for the operator.
- Give your name and phone number.
- Do *not* hang up until instructed to do so by the operator.
- After the call, notify your supervisor and/or other key personnel.
- Make sure someone meets the responders and guides them to the appropriate location.
- Do *not* move injured people unless it is absolutely necessary. If medical providers are available, let them decide whether to move anyone who has been hurt or administer other emergency first aid.
- Let the responders do their job once they arrive.
- Document your actions.
- After the event is over, talk with your supervisor and coworkers about how the response went and how it could be better next time.

SPECIFIC SITUATIONS:

A POTENTIALLY SUICIDAL CLIENT

Suicide is one of the top ten causes of death in the United States, and having a mental health or substance-use disorder is one of the most powerful predictors of suicide, suicide attempts, and suicidal thoughts. Peers are very likely to have contact with people who are suicidal, and so will want to seek out training and supervisor guidance on how to deal with this common and critical situation.

If you think someone may be suicidal, contact your supervisor or another available clinician as quickly as possible. Clinical providers often have significant training in assessing and responding to suicidal adults. Get them involved quickly and follow their guidance.

However, it's not always easy to know if a client is suicidal. Someone may need to ask the person for more information before it becomes clear that he or she is at risk. Talk with your supervisor about whether you should notify them immediately or first ask questions of the client directly on your own.

Watch for some of the following common warning signs:

- Talking about suicide.
- Getting the means to commit suicide.
- Being preoccupied with death.
- Withdrawing from social contact; wanting to be left alone.
- Feeling trapped or hopeless.
- Engaging in risky or self-destructive behaviors.
- Increasing substance use.
- Giving away belongings; getting affairs in order for death.

If you are going to speak with the client before seeking out a supervisor or other clinician, ask clear, simple questions:

- "Do you feel like giving up?"
- "Do you think a lot about dying?"
- "Have you been having thoughts about hurting yourself?"
- "Have you thought about how you might hurt yourself?"
- "Do you have the means of hurting yourself available to you?"

If you believe the client is actively suicidal:

- Do not leave the person alone—stay engaged with him or her.
- Get help as quickly as possible. Call a supervisor, 911, or the police, depending on how critical the situation is and who is immediately available to you.
- Keep the person engaged while help is coming.
- Encourage the person to get help.
- Offer to go with the person to get help.
- Be respectful of the person's feelings. Don't be judgmental or patronizing.

A POTENTIALLY HOMICIDAL OR VIOLENT CLIENT

Violence occurs in many work settings, including mental health settings. Training and preparation are critical for recognizing potential risks and preventing violent incidents.

If you think someone has the potential for violence in the near future, contact your supervisor or another available clinician immediately. Again, clinical providers typically have significant training in assessing and responding to potential violence. Get them involved quickly.

It's not always easy to recognize if someone has the potential to be violent in the near future. That's why it is important to take the following common precautions in all settings.

- If you work in a specific area, think about how to make the area safer. For example, make sure you have a way to leave safely if someone becomes threatening. Keep the space relatively uncluttered—eliminate items that someone could use to hurt you or others.
- Have ways to get help quickly, and know how to use them (e.g., panic buttons or alarms).
- Talk with coworkers and supervisors in your area about how you can work together to respond to a potentially violent situation.
- Know how to access security and police officials quickly. Talk with them about working together for safety.
- Request a formal assessment of safety by a licensed professional.

A SITUATION THAT INVOLVES POSSIBLE INTIMATE PARTNER VIOLENCE OR DOMESTIC ABUSE

Intimate partner violence (IPV) refers to physical or sexual violence, threats, or emotional abuse between people who have or have had an intimate relationship. Accurate data about IPV is difficult to collect, but at least 30 percent of women and 10 percent of men will experience IPV in their lifetimes.

Learn and follow the local guidelines for responding to these situations. Talk about them with your supervisor before you uncover actual situations and have to respond.

If you think you are working with someone involved in a violent relationship, or if you think it is likely there is violence, contact your supervisor or another available clinician as quickly as possible. As stated before, clinical providers often have significant training in identifying, assessing, and responding to violence.

It's often not easy to tell if someone is experiencing IPV, and many people are hesitant to talk about it. Watch for some of the most common warning signs that may identify victims of IPV:

- They appear overly afraid of or anxious to please their partner.
- They may talk about their partner's temper or possessive or controlling nature.
- They frequently make excuses for their partner's behavior and negative treatment of them.
- They may have a series of injuries, with vague or suspicious excuses.
- They may frequently miss work or school, again with vague or suspicious excuses.
- They may be isolated from friends or family. They may rarely see others besides their partner.

The full range of warning signs of IPV, including signs that you are working with someone who may be violent with their partner, is beyond the scope of this pocket resource. Talk with your supervisor about learning more about this topic.

A SITUATION THAT INVOLVES POSSIBLE CHILD ABUSE

Child abuse is common, and can include physical, sexual, or emotional abuse or neglect. Estimates suggest that in the United States, five children die every day as a result of child abuse.

Learn and follow the local guidelines for responding to the discovery of child abuse. Talk about them with your supervisor before you uncover situations and have to respond.

Every state in the U.S. has laws mandating professionals to report evidence of child abuse that they become aware of. Common mandated reporters include physicians, social workers, psychologists, counselors, teachers, and police. Peer Support Specialists and other people who may not be mandated to report child abuse can report it. Talk with your supervisor and local providers about how to handle situations in which you become aware of possible or likely child abuse. Again, clinical providers often have significant training in assessing and responding to child abuse. Get them involved quickly.

There is a wide range of warning signs of child abuse—a discussion of all of the signs is beyond the scope of this pocket resource. Talk with your supervisor to learn more.

A SITUATION THAT INVOLVES POSSIBLE ELDER ABUSE

Abuse of older adults is also surprisingly common and involves physical, sexual, or emotional abuse, as well as neglect or abandonment, or misuse of the older adult's money or property. Elder abuse can happen in families or in institutions that care for the elderly. Learn and follow the local and regional guidelines for responding to elder abuse. Talk about them with your supervisor before you uncover situations and have to respond. Similar to child-abuse laws, there are regional laws mandating healthcare professionals to report elder abuse. If you think you are working with someone who might be a victim of elder abuse, contact your supervisor or another available clinician as quickly as possible. Watch for some of the most common warning signs that may identify victims of elder abuse:

- They may seem depressed or confused.
- They are losing weight for no reason.
- They have trouble sleeping.
- They act agitated or violent.
- They have become withdrawn.
- They stop taking part in activities enjoyed in the past.
- They have unexplained bruises, burns, or scars.
- They look messy; they may have unwashed hair or dirty clothes.
- They display signs of trauma (i.e., rocking back and forth).
- They develop bedsores or other preventable conditions.

APPENDIX B: SUGGESTED ANSWERS FOR EXERCISES

Note there are many good answers to these exercises. These suggested answers meet the criteria for a good answer. To evaluate your answers, look at these examples and the criteria for success.

EXERCISE 3: LISTENING FOR THOUGHTS, FEELINGS AND ACTIONS (CHAPTER 7)

For each of the following statements from a hypothetical client, write down what you are hearing in each of the three categories. Try to get all of the content they are sharing without adding more than they are actually saying

---

1. "I'm really glad you are willing to talk with me. I asked my doctor to refer me to a peer counselor, but they just ignored me. It makes me so mad that they don't pay any attention to what I want. I don't really even talk to them any more—I just skip most of my appointments. If they are not going to listen to me, why should I listen to them?"

What do you hear about their thoughts?
They think their doctor does not listen to them and that this is a clear pattern that is not going to change. Given the doctor's behavior, they see no reason to listen to the doctor.

What do you hear about their feelings?
They are angry at the doctor. They feel hopeless about this changing. They are not going to listen to the doctor as a way to get back at them.

What do you hear about their actions?
They asked for a referral to a peer counselor. They have skipped most of their appointments. They don't want to listen to the doctor and may have stopped listening already.

<table>
<tr><td>

2. "Are you a peer counselor? My psychologist said I was supposed to meet with you, but they didn't say why. I guess they thought I needed more help than I was getting. They didn't say it, but I think I'm getting more and more depressed. They are probably worried that I'll do something stupid."

</td></tr>
<tr><td>

What do you hear about their thoughts?
They think their psychologist referred them to you because the psychologist thinks the client is getting more depressed, is not getting enough support, and may "do something stupid."

</td></tr>
<tr><td>

What do you hear about their feelings?
They feel concerned that their psychologist thinks they are getting worse—getting more depressed. They feel unclear why they were referred to the Peer Support Specialist. They feel discouraged about getting worse.

</td></tr>
<tr><td>

What do you hear about their actions?
They don't say anything about their actions, but raise the issue of whether they might do something "stupid," which likely refers to something self-destructive or at least impulsive.

</td></tr>
</table>

<table>
<tr><td>

3. "I went to my first AA meeting last night—it was actually pretty good! I met a very nice person who was also there for the first time—they were VERY nice. We sat together during the meeting and hung out afterward. I think I could fit into that group. I didn't say anything in the meeting, but I liked what I heard. I plan to go again next week."

</td></tr>
<tr><td>

What do you hear about their thoughts?
They are surprised by how good the meeting was. They liked at least one person and think they could fit into the group. They plan to attend again.

</td></tr>
<tr><td>

What do you hear about their feelings?
They are surprised that they liked the group. They liked the other new person they met—particularly at how "nice" they were. They feel excited about finding the group and participating in the group in the future.

</td></tr>
<tr><td>

What do you hear about their actions?
They attended their first AA meeting the night before. They didn't say anything, but listened to others. They met and talked to another new person and connected with them. They plan to attend next week.

</td></tr>
</table>

EXERCISE 4: REFLECTIONS (CHAPTER 8)

For each of the following statements from a hypothetical client, write at least one possible reflection for each of the four categories (simple, feelings, thoughts, actions).

---

1. **"I've got to go to court tomorrow for a DUI. I'm not sure what is going to happen—I've never done this before. Could be really bad."**

Simple reflection: You are worried how it will go tomorrow at court related to this DUI.

Reflecting the feelings: This court date tomorrow is totally new to you. You are worried what will happen.

Reflecting the thoughts: You don't know what to think about your court date tomorrow, since you've never been in this situation before. You think there is a significant risk of a bad outcome for you.

Reflecting the actions: Tomorrow, you have to go to court. You have to walk into a situation that is totally new for you and there is a real risk of something bad.

---

2. **"My nurse said I'm not losing weight fast enough. I don't think they believe me that I'm doing all of the exercises, but I am! Losing weight has always been really hard for me—you'd think they would understand that."**

Simple reflection: Your nurse said your weight is not changing quickly enough. You think they don't believe you are working hard enough and they don't understand how this works for you.

Reflecting the feelings: You feel frustrated that they don't believe you—that you are not being honest about what you are doing, even though you are.

Reflecting the thoughts: Your nurse said you are not losing weight quickly enough and you think that means they don't think you are doing your exercises. You think they don't understand how difficult this is for you.

Reflecting the actions: You have been doing all of the exercises. They say you are not progressing as fast and they think you should. This has always been hard for you.

3. **"My doctor referred me to this cancer support group at the hospital. I went and there were only four people there and they were all really old. They looked really sick too—I'm not that sick! It was depressing! I can't relate to them—what a waste of my time."**

Simple reflection: You went to the support group your doctor suggested, but the few members that were there were very different from you. It felt depressing and you don't see the value.

Reflecting the feelings: You didn't feel like the group members were like you, and they looked very sick. It was alarming and depressing.

Reflecting the thoughts: You thought the group members were older and sicker than you and so different that you can't relate to them. You think the group is not worth attending.

Reflecting the actions: You followed your doctor's suggestions and went to this group. They seemed pretty different than you and you feel you won't be able to relate to them. Sounds like you are not going to go again.

EXERCISE 5: SUMMARY STATEMENTS (CHAPTER 9)

For each of the following statements from a hypothetical client, write a summary statement. Remember that good summary statements are usually shorter than the client's comments, but organize those comments in a useful way.

<table>
<tr><td>

1. "My medications are making me sleep better, which is something good. When I can't sleep at least six hours a night, I can't think clearly the next day and then I feel depressed. I've had three nights of good sleep in a row—that is the best in months! Maybe I could stop talking to the psychologist if I just got my sleep all settled. I don't like those talking sessions. They just make me feel tense afterward."

</td></tr>
<tr><td>

Write a possible summary statement for your client.

Your medications are helping you sleep, and that is helping you feel less depressed. You are feeling so good that you are considering stopping your psychotherapy. You don't like the therapy and it seems to make you feel more tense instead of better.

</td></tr>
</table>

<table>
<tr><td>

2. "My parents don't have much money and so I can't get the treatment I really need. I have no insurance and I haven't worked for a year. I can't imagine I can get over this anxiety without good treatment, but I can't afford it. I'm sure everyone else in this day treatment program here has good insurance. I bet I'm going to have to drop out."

</td></tr>
<tr><td>

Write a possible summary statement for your client.

You don't have a lot of resources including health insurance. You are worried that without treatment you won't get better. You think you may have to drop out.

</td></tr>
</table>

3. "When my wife died, I lost everything. She was the center of my world. I had no friends. I couldn't stay in that house—it was too depressing. I moved here near my daughter in order to try to start over, but I don't know how to do that. I sit in my apartment all day alone—I can't stand it. I don't think my daughter understands what this is like. Maybe I should sign up for a dating app."

Write a possible summary statement for your client.

You feel really lost since your wife died. You moved out here hoping it would help, but you are very isolated. Your daughter doesn't seem to understand. You think maybe a dating app would help this.

EXERCISE 6: ADVANCED REFLECTIONS AND SUMMARIES (CHAPTER 18).

For each of the following statements from a hypothetical client, write down at least two possible advanced reflections. Be sure to include content that you think is likely true but is beyond what the client actually said.

<table>
<tr><td colspan="2">1. Your client is talking about a close friend who treats them poorly. They say this is a pattern over many years. Your client says they want to confront their friend but doesn't feel "ready."

You think that your client is not saying that they have very few friends and feel lonely often.</td></tr>
<tr><td>Possible Advanced Reflection #1</td><td>You want to confront your friend about the way they treat you. You don't have a lot of friends, and you are worried you might lose one of the few you have.</td></tr>
<tr><td>Possible Advanced Reflection #2</td><td>You are pretty alone these days. You don't feel ready to confront your friend, given it may cost you one of the few social contacts you have. When would you feel "ready"?</td></tr>
</table>

<table>
<tr><td>2. Your client is talking about feeling a great deal of stomach pain over the past three weeks. They don't know what is causing it, but they have not called their doctor.

What you think is also true but your client is not saying: Their mother died of stomach cancer around the same age. Your client nursed her mother for the last months of her life and describes it as a "terrible experience."</td></tr>
</table>

Possible Advanced Reflection #1	You have a lot of pain but haven't talked with your doctor about it. I'm wondering if this is reminding you of your mother's cancer and that scares you enough to keep from taking action.
Possible Advanced Reflection #2	You are kind of frozen in the face of this bad stomach pain. What do you think it might mean? You talked before about your mother—is there a link to what you saw at the end of her life and how you feel now?

3. Your client is talking about returning to weekly meetings of Alcoholics Anonymous. They stopped going when they started dating their new girlfriend.

What you think is also true but your client is not saying: Your client has not told their girlfriend about their past problems with alcohol. They feel embarrassed about letting anyone know about this problem.

Possible Advanced Reflection #1	You are planning on going back to AA. I was surprised you stopped going, given how important it was for you. You started dating your girlfriend around that time—that can make it difficult to talk openly about AA and your past.
Possible Advanced Reflection #2	You feel ready to head back to AA. Does that mean you feel ready to bring this up with your girlfriend now? You kind of split that part of your life off from your relationship with her.

4. Your client is talking about wanting to change psychiatrists. "Dr. White never listens to me. He's always pushing me to take medications. I don't think he likes me." What you think is also true but your client is not saying: Your client was very stable on medications in the past and recently stopped taking any medications. Since that time, they have been complaining about symptoms and associated problems at work.	
Possible Advanced Reflection #1	You've used medications successfully in the past. You stopped and then your symptoms got worse and your problems at work got worse. Now you don't like working with your prescriber. Seems like this is all connected and is going in a concerning direction.
Possible Advanced Reflection #2	You are in bad spot. You don't want to take medications and have stepped away from them. Since then, your symptoms are worse—which may be why Dr. White is pushing you. Can you see why he might be doing that? Other psychiatrists are likely to say the same thing. What do you want to happen?

EXERCISE 7: CHALLENGING THOUGHTS AND ACTIONS (CHAPTER 96).

For each of the following scenarios from a hypothetical client, write a challenge at the low, moderate, and high levels of assertiveness.

1. The client has complained to you repeatedly about how their husband is not honest about his feelings. They just described to you a situation in which *they* are not being honest about their feelings with their husband.	
Low Assertiveness	You don't feel comfortable being direct about your feelings with your husband. You've mentioned that he doesn't seem to feel comfortable at times either.
Moderate Assertiveness	You don't feel comfortable being direct about your feelings with your husband. That is very remarkable in that you've often accused him of the very same thing.
High Assertiveness	Do you hear how you are the one who is not honest in this situation? You often complain about this for your husband but you are doing it now. What is that about, do you think?

2. You hear from a clinical team member that your client has relapsed on alcohol. You have been talking with this client for months about their cravings and how to manage them. They come to see you but don't mention their relapse, presenting themselves as "doing well".	
Low Assertiveness	So, you know that I'm on your clinical team and we all share information about clients as part of treatment. I did hear from Dr. Johnson recently. I am curious that you've not brought up your recent relapse.
Moderate Assertiveness	So, you know that I'm on your clinical team and we all share information about clients as part of treatment. I did hear from Dr. Johnson recently. I am concerned that you've not brought up your recent relapse. You are acting like it didn't happen. That surprises me.
High Assertiveness	We've been talking together for months now. It seems like we've built up a lot of trust, working together about your cravings and recovery. I did hear from Dr. Johnson recently about your relapse. I'm concerned that you have not brought that up to me. I thought we were partners and that there was openness and trust in our work together. How has that broken down?

3. Your client has been talking with you for weeks about their desire to have more friends to address their intense feelings of loneliness. It is their primary goal for peer counseling. Today they told you about some new people who are living in their building. When you ask if they have talked to them, your client says, "I am not really interested in talking to other people."

Low Assertiveness	That is a little surprising. I thought you've been saying for a while that you wanted to have more friends and feel less lonely.
Moderate Assertiveness	That is very curious. You say you don't want to talk with other people, but we've been working on that for weeks now. I don't really understand. Can you help me understand how those statements fit together?
High Assertiveness	That sounds like an excuse for avoiding new people. You've been working for weeks on making new friends. Now that there is a good chance, you say you don't want them. You are not being honest with yourself or with me right now.

4. Your client regularly attends a peer support group. They complain to you every week about the group meetings, saying that they want the group to talk more about tension in the group. You ask your client if they have ever brought up the topic. They say, "I don't want to bring that topic up. Someone else should do it!"	
Low Assertiveness	Sounds like a dangerous group. No one feels comfortable talking about the tensions.
Moderate Assertiveness	Sounds like this must be a fairly dangerous group. No one feels comfortable talking about the tensions. What makes you all so afraid to talk frankly?
High Assertiveness	So, you want everyone else to bring it up but you can't do what you want them to do. You don't feel comfortable talking about the tension in the group and neither does anyone else. What could be so dangerous that no one will bring this up?

REFERENCES

Allday, R. A., & Pakurar, K. (2007). Effects of teacher greetings on student on-task behavior. *Journal of Applied Behavior Analysis, 40*(2), 317-320.

Artiga, S., Orgera, K., & Pham, O. (2020). Disparities in health and health care: Five key questions and answers. *Kaiser Family Foundation.*

Bridges, A. J., de Arellano, M. A., Rheingold, A. A., Danielson, C. K., & Silcott, L. (2010). Trauma exposure, mental health, and service utilization rates among immigrant and United States-born Hispanic youth: Results from the Hispanic family study. *Psychological Trauma: Theory, Research, Practice, And Policy, 2*(1), 40.

Byhoff, E., Guardado, R., Xiao, N., Nokes, K., Garg, A., & Tripodis, Y. (2022). Association of unmet social needs with chronic illness: a cross-sectional study. *Population Health Management, 25*(2), 157-163.

Cruwys, T., Wakefield, J. R., Sani, F., Dingle, G. A., & Jetten, J. (2018). Social isolation predicts frequent attendance in primary care. *Annals of Behavioral Medicine, 52*(10), 817-829.

Eisenberg, D., Gollust, S. E., Golberstein, E., & Hefner, J. L. (2007). Prevalence and correlates of depression, anxiety, and suicidality among university students. *American Journal of Orthopsychiatry, 77*(4), 534-542.

Evans-Lacko, S., Henderson, C., & Thornicroft, G. (2013). Public knowledge, attitudes and behaviour regarding people with mental illness in England 2009-2012. *The British Journal of Psychiatry, 202*(s55), s51-s57.

Finlayson Smith, A. (2007). Do clients want their spiritual and religious beliefs to be discussed in therapy? *Psychotherapy in Australia, 14*(1), 56-9.

Fischer, E. P., McSweeney, J. C., Wright, P., Cheney, A., Curran, G. M., Henderson, K., & Fortney, J. C. (2016). Overcoming barriers to sustained engagement in mental health care: perspectives of rural veterans and providers. *The Journal of Rural Health, 32*(4), 429-438.

Galinsky, A. M., Zelaya, C. E., Barnes, P. M., & Simile, C. (2022). Selected health conditions among native Hawaiian and Pacific Islander adults: United States, 2014. *Cancer, 23*, 2.

Georgetown Health Policy Institute (2024, January 24) Cultural Competence in Health Care: Is it important for people with chronic conditions? https://hpi.georgetown.edu/cultural/.

Hauenstein, E. J., Petterson, S., Merwin, E., Rovnyak, V., Heise, B., & Wagner, D. (2006). Rurality, gender, and mental health treatment. *Family and Community Health*, 169-185.

Henderson, R. C., Williams, P., Gabbidon, J., Farrelly, S., Schauman, O., Hatch, S., . . . & MIRIAD Study Group. (2015). Mistrust of mental health services: ethnicity, hospital admission and unfair treatment. *Epidemiology and Psychiatric Sciences, 24*(3), 258-265.

Holt-Lunstad, J., Smith, T. B., Baker, M., Harris, T., & Stephenson, D. (2015). Loneliness and social isolation as risk factors for mortality: a meta-analytic review. *Perspectives on Psychological Science, 10*(2), 227-237.

Houlston, C., Smith, P.K., & Jessel, J. (2011). "The relationship between use of school-based peer support initiatives and the social and emotional well-being of bullied and non-bullied students." *Children and Society 25*, 293-305.

Jones, D. S. (2006). The persistence of American Indian health disparities. *American Journal of Public Health, 96*(12), 2122-2134.

Kaskutas, L. (2009). "Alcoholics Anonymous effectiveness: faith meets science." *Journal of Addictive Diseases, 28*, 145-157.

Kelly, J. F., Stout, R. L., Magill, M., Tonigan, J.S., & Pagano, M.E. (2010). "Mechanisms of behavior change in Alcoholics Anonymous: Does AA improve alcohol outcomes by reducing depression symptoms?" *Addiction, 105*, 626-636.

Kennedy, A., Reeves, D., Bower, P., Lee, V., Middleton, E., Richardson, G., Garner, C., Gatley, C., &. Rogers, A. (2007). "The effectiveness and cost effectiveness of a national lay-led self-care support programme for patients with long-term conditions: a pragmatic randomized controlled trial." *Journal of Epidemiology and Community Health, 61*: 254-26.

Lepkowski, W. J., Packman, J., Smaby, M. H., & Maddux, C. (2009). Comparing self and expert assessments of counseling skills before and after skills training, and upon graduation. *Education, 129*(3), 363-372.

Molinsky, A. (2016). The 4 Types of Ineffective Apologies. *Harvard Business Review*, Extracted 1/23/2024 https://hbr.org/2016/11/the-4-types-of-ineffective-apologiesThe 4 Types of Ineffective Apologies (hbr.org).

Mustanski, B. S., Garofalo, R., & Emerson, E. M. (2010). Mental health disorders, psychological distress, and suicidality in a diverse sample of lesbian, gay, bisexual, and transgender youths. *American Journal of Public Health, 100*(12), 2426-2432.

National Association of Peer Supporters (2019). *National Practice Guidelines for Peer Specialists and Supervisors*. Washington, DC: N.A.P.S.

Olsson, S., Hensing, G., Burström, B., & Löve, J. (2021). Unmet need for mental healthcare in a population sample in Sweden: a cross-sectional study of inequalities based on gender, education, and country of birth. *Community Mental Health Journal, 57*(3), 470-481.

Pagano, M. E., White, W. L., Kelly, J. F., Stout, R. L., Carter, R. R., & Tonigan, J.S. (2013). The 10-year course of AA participation and long-term outcomes: A follow-up study of outpatient subjects in Project MATCH. *Substance Abuse, 34(1),* 51-59.

Rakoczy, H. (2022). Foundations of theory of mind and its development in early childhood. *Nature Reviews Psychology, 1*(4), 223-235.

Rowe, M. (2008). Micro-affirmations and micro inequities. *Journal of the International Ombudsman Association, 1*, 45–48.

Culture Definition & Meaning - Merriam-Webster, Extracted 1/23/2024.

Steele, L., Dewa, C., & Lee, K. (2007). Socioeconomic status and self-reported barriers to mental health service use. *The Canadian Journal of Psychiatry, 52*(3), 201-206.

Sullivan-Baca, E., Rehman, R., & Haneef, Z. (2023). An update on the healthy soldier effect in US Veterans. *Military Medicine, 188*(9-10), 3199-3204.

Tervalon, M., & Murray-Garcia, J. (1998). Cultural humility versus cultural competence: A critical distinction in defining physician training outcomes in multicultural education. *Journal of Health Care for the Poor and Underserved, 9*(2), 117-125.

Thompson, M. N., Goldberg, S. B., & Nielsen, S. L. (2018). Patient financial distress and treatment outcomes in naturalistic psychotherapy. *Journal of Counseling Psychology, 65*(4), 523.

Topor, A., Bøe, T. D., & Larsen, I. B. (2018). Small things, micro-affirmations and helpful professionals' everyday recovery-orientated practices according to persons with mental health problems. *Community Mental Health Journal, 54*, 1212-1220.

Walker, E. R., Cummings, J. R., Hockenberry, J. M., & Druss, B. G. (2015). Insurance status, use of mental health services, and unmet need for mental health care in the United States. *Psychiatric Services, 66*(6), 578-584.

Yang, K. G., Rodgers, C. R., Lee, E., & Lê Cook, B. (2020). Disparities in mental health care utilization and perceived need among Asian Americans: 2012–2016. *Psychiatric Services, 71*(1), 21-27.